# PRAISE FOR *THE JOURNEY OF AN OLD WHITE DUDE IN THE AGE OF BLACK LIVES MATTER: A PRIMER*

"*The Journey of an Old White Dude* is a distinguished, provocative, and essential work that teaches how to effectively address modern racial challenges in a way that few works do—and can. A deep bow to John Gerdy for his unabashed vulnerability, sheer courage, and studious diligence, and, by dint of his remarkable personal path and impactful social contributions, being a role model for us all."

—Michael J. Coffino, Award-Winning Author of *Truth Is in the House*

"A work of concise and explanatory nuggets clearly dissecting the toughest issues of race, gender, justice, and equity . . . appreciatively digested because Gerdy's delivery is devoid of diatribe, guilt, and chastisement and artfully culled from history and the words and thoughts of wise men and women. He simply expresses lessons learned through his personal experiences and the privileged lens of a thoughtful White man who happens to be extraordinarily gifted athlete, musician, and communicator. Most of all, the reader will be captivated by a master storyteller—an educator through and through. The best teachers are performing artists of a special sort, and Gerdy is one of these."

—Dr. Donna Lopiano, President, Sports Management Resources, Former CEO of the Women's Sports Foundation, Former Director of Women's Athletics at the University of Texas, Austin

"John Gerdy's lived experiences as a player, athletic administrator, and scholar-activist give him a unique perspective on race relations in this country. The context of sport, and more specifically basketball, helped shape this perspective and further afforded him a platform to engage the critical subject matter of race. His transition or evolution to founding the Music For Everyone (MFE) nonprofit is an extension of his social justice efforts. This is an honest account of how racial blinders, bloopers, and blunders as an 'old White dude' and founder of MFE created opportunities for reflection, introspection, and transformation.

"In this era where anti-Black racism is pervasive and weaponized to justify the killing of unarmed Black men and women, 'old White dudes,' who dominate the political machinery in this country, need to read and listen to this 'old White dude.' When anti-critical race theory storm troopers, mainly 'old White dudes,' seek to make America great again through the whitewashing of American history and denying a critical interrogation of 'old White dudes'' interpretation of it, this 'old White dude' has something to say.

"[Gerdy] tackles some tough racial issues and contributes to the dialogue on race. He gives nuggets to address some of these protracted racial issues that continue to challenge this nation.

"Whether you seek to develop a social justice orientation or you are an advocate or activist for social justice, you could benefit, and therefore, I recommend you read this 'old White dude.'"

—Dr. Billy Hawkins, Professor of Health and Human Performance at the University of Houston, Author of *The New Plantation: Black Athletes, College Sports, and Predominantly White NCAA Institutions*

"*The Journey of an Old White Dude in the Age of Black Lives Matter: A Primer* is a must-read—not only for 'old White dudes' but for anyone who has a spark of humanity and feels morally obligated to seek social justice. This book provides a space for White readers who wish to be informed allies to come face-to-face with their privilege and do the hard work of becoming more informed. Dr. Gerdy has challenged himself as he challenges us. I highly recommend this book."

—Dr. Richard Southall, Director, College Sport Research Institute; Professor, Department of Sport & Entertainment Management, University of South Carolina

"When John Gerdy showed up at the SEC meetings in the late '80s as a young administrator, I was immediately impressed. He was bright, witty, confident, and understood the proper role of athletics in college life as well as anyone I had ever known. As a jock, I would have been even more impressed had I known he was Davidson's all-time leading scorer in basketball (pre-Steph Curry, of course)!

"Naturally, we hit it off. We talked about creating the right kind of environment for student-athletes, an atmosphere that adhered to the standards needed to insure each one of an opportunity to get a real college education while competing at the highest level in his/her sport. We discussed ways to implement real diversity, encouraging team building in every area, especially between those with racial, religious, and ethnic differences. John worked hard against considerable resistance and made a real difference.

"Here is what John Gerdy said to us coaches in the SEC by his actions and plans: 'Folks, how about trying something new. Let's actually be who we say we are!'

"Now in his book, *The Journey of an Old White Dude in the Age of Black Lives Matter: A Primer*, John eloquently challenges each of us, especially other old White dudes, to consider the same. I hope many, many readers are exposed to the thorough scholarship in John's compelling work. How great our country would be if we actually become who we say we are!"

—Bill Curry, Two-Time Super Bowl Champion,
Longtime College Football Coach

"Racial justice is the issue of our generation. As a fellow 'old White dude,' I have traveled a similar journey as John. His words are meaningful, his stories relatable, and his message vital in this time. John's message is prescient for those who want to play a role in bending the arc of the moral universe towards justice. He invites those who may not have been aware, either willfully or ignorantly, to open their hearts and minds to the lived experiences of our friends, neighbors, and colleagues of color. As we walk through this time, burdened with unjust vestiges of the past, John's words offer a glimpse of a more just future for all and will inspire readers to seek that justice in their communities. The truth in the book is palpable. So, yes, *The Journey of an Old White Dude in the Age of Black Lives Matter* will inevitably be banned in America's most fragile communities."

—Samuel Bressi, President and CEO, Lancaster County Community Foundation

"An exceptional work that says it like it is and says it straight: the color of our hide is screwed up in our psyches. The pus in our America boil . . . [is] racism, and lancing it is our work. Gerdy has provided a powerful recipe to do that."

—David Meggyesy, Seven-Year NFL Linebacker, Author of *Out of Their League,* NFLPA, Western Regional Director, Co-Founder of Esalen Sports Center, Athletes United for Peace, and Evolutionary Sports Collective

"Here Gerdy disarmingly embraces his imperfections, mines his considerable organizational experience, and compels his readers to do the necessary work to counter White privilege and move the needle towards greater racial justice in America.

"Drawing on sports, American history, music, current events, and recent literature on race, he offers sound guidance for White Americans to go beneath the surface, and to the heart of the matter, to confront racial injustice in our daily lives."

—Thomas R. Ryan, PhD, President and CEO, LancasterHistory

"John Gerdy risks putting his White privilege on display to speak to the systemic racism currently plaguing our society. While we can agree he has a point of view that is shared with so many of his generation, his book is also a plea for change and understanding, believing that open dialogue is the way forward. As an educator who came from a family of educators, together with the multiple programs he has initiated and sponsored, his intent is clear: beginning with old White dudes such as himself, we must all do better.

"Gerdy expresses his vision using facts interlaced with enlightening storytelling about such topics as the role of athletics in our schools, the universal nature of art and music's educational effectiveness, and the enrichment to businesses when they include POC as part of their team. The reader gains abundant insight into why he has taken this position and so adamantly wants others to join him on his crusade for truth and justice.

"I commend John's effort and hope this book is far-reaching and will indeed help effect positive change."

—Teri Rider, CEO, Top Reads Publishing

"Dr. John Gerdy has been researching and contributing to the academy for over thirty years. This book is provocative, insightful, and captures the true essence of our forever changing society. This is a must-read."

—Dr. Fritz G. Polite, Associate VP, Shenandoah University

*The Journey of an Old White Dude in the Age of Black Lives Matter: A Primer*

by John R. Gerdy

Published by

 köehlerbooks™

3705 Shore Drive
Virginia Beach, VA 23455
800-435-4811
www.koehlerbooks.com

# THE **JOURNEY** OF AN **OLD WHITE DUDE** IN THE AGE OF **BLACK LIVES MATTER**

## *A Primer*

## JOHN R. GERDY

VIRGINIA BEACH
CAPE CHARLES

# OTHER BOOKS BY JOHN R. GERDY

*The Successful College Athletics Program: The New Standard*

*Sports in School: The Future of an Institution*

*Sports: The All-American Addiction*

*Air Ball: American Education's Failed Experiment with Elite Athletics*

*Ball or Bands: Football vs. Music as an Educational
and Community Investment*

*The AlphaBone Orchestra: A Magically Musical Journey
Through the Alpahabet*

*Lights on Lancaster: How One American City Harnesses the Power of
the Arts to Transform its Communities
(Release date October, 2023)*

*To Wallace and James,*

*Thank you for encouraging me to write this book.*
*My hope is that it moves the needle towards a more just and tolerant*
*world that you and your generation can build upon.*

A portion of the proceeds from the sale of this book will be donated to the Lancaster Chapter of the NAACP and the Lancaster Bail Fund

To learn more about Music For Everyone and the Songs For Justice project, please visit: MusicForEveryone.net

To learn more about John, please visit: JohnGerdy.com

# TABLE OF CONTENTS

# PREFACE

*"We continue to love a country that doesn't love us back".*

—Glenn "Doc" Rivers, NBA Basketball Coach and Future Hall of Famer (August 25, 2020)

I am an Old White Dude.

As such, who am I to speak or write about social justice, racial equity, or what being a person of color (POC) in America is like? I am a product of White privilege. I grew up in a segregated town and went to overwhelmingly White schools, and while I have friends who are Black, they don't comprise a large segment of my inner circle. In short, I'm like the vast majority of Old White Dudes in America. What do I know about this stuff? It's a fair question.

To the young, "being old" means being "out of touch," antiquated, close-minded, backwards, and outdated in beliefs. I know this because a popular mantra of my generation was, "Don't trust anyone over forty."

Ah, the circle of life. Now I am the one out of touch. I am the one not to be trusted.

But "old" also means you have accumulated many experiences and have had more time and opportunity to observe, contemplate, and absorb many of life's lessons, mysteries, contradictions, and challenges. There's a difference between being "old" and "being old." Old is simply a number. Being old is an attitude, a mindset that can resist change and be closed to new and different ideas and experiences.

At my advanced age, I have no time to "be old."

I am well aware that I do not *really* know the tribulations of being Black in America. Not even close. I don't have to worry about getting shot during a traffic stop or getting followed by wary shop keepers while browsing a gift store. Nor did I have to give my kids "The Talk" that every Black parent must give to their children about how to survive encounters with police. In short, while I may have walked alongside POC, I have never walked in their shoes. To imply otherwise would be insulting.

Once again, this begs the question: "Who am I to write this book?"

Simply because I am not Black does not mean I don't have relevant experiences, observations, ideas, or thoughts that have shaped my beliefs and defined my values regarding racism and diversity. It does not mean that I haven't thought about and been committed to the cause of justice and equity. While I may be an Old White Dude, I have always been aware of, sensitive to, and thought a lot about issues of race.

It began with my parents. Discrimination and prejudice of any sort was simply not allowed in our household. Intolerance was not tolerated. Period.

Pretty easy, huh?

Not quite!

If it were that easy, there'd be no reason to write this book or for any of the other dozens of books written about race in America. I mention this simply to mark a starting point, for what became a lifelong awareness of, interest in, and commitment to issues around race, justice, and equity, with particular application to fair access to educational opportunity.

I enjoyed a long and reasonably successful career as a basketball player, which resulted in All-State and All-American honors, and a year as a professional. I've also represented our country in international competition. My high school (Passaic Valley in Little Falls, New Jersey) and college (Davidson College) honored me by retiring my jersey number, which now hangs in the rafters of their respective arenas. I held Davidson's career scoring mark for thirty years before Steph Curry came along. In short, I had a pretty good run at a world class level.

Basketball culture is Black dominated. Thus, I often found myself in positions of being a minority. I had to observe and negotiate the mores, subtleties, and nuances of an unfamiliar culture to succeed as a player and teammate. That was because my Black teammates greatly influenced team culture and mores. In all other situations in which I found myself, White men made all the rules.

Later, as a college athletic administrator at both the National Collegiate Athletic Association (NCAA) and the Southeastern Conference (SEC), as a non-profit administrator (Music For Everyone) (MFE), and in books and numerous writings and essays, my work centered on access to educational opportunity, particularly as it applies to POC. In the case of college athletics, it was the educational and economic exploitation of the Black athlete and with MFE, access to music education opportunities for predominantly minority populations.

That journey led me to Music For Everyone's Songs For Justice (SFJ) project, which will be used here as a vehicle to highlight those issues. MFE is a non-profit organization I founded in 2006 with a mission to cultivate the power of music as an educational and community-building tool in Lancaster County, PA. I use the SFJ project to speak to my fellow Old White Dudes about the responsibilities, challenges, and, most important, the opportunities that exist for Old White Dudes in the Age of Black Lives Matter.

Now that I have answered the "who," what about the "why?" Why did I write this book?

I've asked myself that question often. I know I am exposing myself to backlash and criticism. Many times, throughout the process of writing, I underwent tremendous self-doubt. I'd ask myself, *With all my White privilege, who do I think I am trying to write about this? What do I really know about this stuff?* In the end, I decided that silence wasn't an option. While I may not be as qualified as others, particularly people of color or professional diversity trainers, to write about race in America, I have meaningful experiences, a thoughtful perspective, and positive intentions. Thus, I had to make the effort. I had to see if I could make a difference and hopefully, inspire others to do the same.

I also felt compelled to write this because, at my core, I am an educator. I come from a family of educators. My father was a high school teacher and football coach, my mother worked in a school system, my sister is a teacher, as is our son. I've taught in pre-school classrooms as well as on college campuses. As an educator, you work hard at researching, gathering, and analyzing information to better understand and place what we learn into a broader context. The more educated we become about issues, the easier it is to teach and spread the word. You educate others in the hope that increased knowledge of history, theories, culture, context, and facts brings increased understanding, empathy, tolerance, and hopefully, action. It also produces increased familiarity and reduced fear of the unknown. I believe that my life experiences, coupled with my work in reading, researching, and contemplating these issues, will benefit others and move the needle of progress forward. That's what educators do.

My hope is that this book strikes a spark of realization and enlightenment, and possibly inspiration for other Old White Dudes. There may also be valuable material and insights for young White dudes, White women, and perhaps even some POC. Hopefully the discussion that follows will contribute to a wider community and societal dialogue. The more voices we hear, the better chance we have of engaging in a wide ranging, societal discussion, which ultimately drives change. But it starts with us Old White Dudes getting our act together. We can do better. We must do better. We can move the needle.

Before moving forward, I want to make four important clarifications. First, there are times when I challenge Old White Dudes (myself included) to get our act together. When I do, however, I am not calling anyone a racist. Are there racists in America? Of course! Are there people who wear their racism as a badge of honor? Of course! Think Ku Klux Klan and the Proud Boys. But I suspect those folks won't be reading this book. Nonetheless, I believe in people's better angels. I believe most people are kind, thoughtful, and want to do the right thing.

The second relates to the book title. Please note the communication line I have drawn between one Old White Dude and other Old White Dudes is simply a rhetorical device. It is not intended to exclude women or, for that matter, young White people from the discussion.

This book is for all White folks and perhaps even some POC who might appreciate the stories, ideas, and perspectives offered.

Next, you probably have already noticed that I capitalize the words *Black* and *White*. Black refers to people who identify as African American or have descended from an African nation. White refers to those who identify as being White American and have cultural or family roots in European countries.

There has been, and continues to be, much debate about when and whether to distinguish Whites and Blacks in this manner. My publisher and I have chosen to follow the guidance of the *Chicago Manual of Style*, which states that its preference, for the purposes of consistency, is to uppercase both Black and White when referring to race or ethnicity. This distinction also acknowledges the long-standing cultural divide between Blacks and Whites in America and elsewhere.

Finally, when referring to Black Lives Matter, I am not referring to the actual BLM organization, but rather the general idea or principle of Black lives actually mattering. In other words, as applied to my usage in these pages, BLM is the movement not the specific BLM organization.

There are many books that cover these topics, most written by people of color. That is as it should be. But there is only so much that Black people can say to White people about these issues. At some point we must create a little extra space for White people to talk about these issues directly with other White people.

That being the case, there is the risk that my phrasing of things may seem insensitive, distorted, tone deaf, disrespectful, or downright clueless to people of color. That is not my intention . . . at all. If I make mistakes, call me out. As the son of a football coach and a former professional athlete, I can take coaching. My goal is not to garner praise from POC. It is to stimulate thought and discussion and to challenge White people to reexamine their understanding and attitudes regarding racism and social justice and, in the end, to inspire attitudinal and behavioral change.

Writing this book has been one of my life's most important and impactful learning experiences. I've learned how enormous the role and influence White privilege has played in my life. As a White man, it is so easy to take that for granted because it has been a constant, touching every part of my life for my entire life. As such, you get used to it… even numb to it. The result is that you rarely think of it.

I've also come to better understand the extent to which Black people have had to deal with and fight the affects and impacts of systemic racism, both big and small. It has literally been a twenty-four hours per day, seven days a week, 365 days a year, for over 400 years battle. I cannot imagine how utterly exhausting it must be to be Black in America.

The process of researching and writing this book involved a lot of self-reflection. As I've come to find, I haven't been as *anti-racist* or as much of a racial *ally* as I thought. I discovered many ways in which I engaged, with no ill intent, in racially insensitive behaviors and patterns. I was forced to confront my own biases, which has been a humbling experience. This is difficult work with enormous challenges. And it is work that lasts for a lifetime, but work that must be done.

It's also been exhilarating. If you approach these issues with profound humility, an open mind, and a commitment to do the necessary work, you can learn. You can grow. You can improve. In that sense, this book is about possibilities, opportunities, and hope.

We are all on a continuum regarding awareness, knowledge of, and commitment to racial justice. For each of us, it is a highly personal journey. My hope is that, wherever you are on that continuum, reading this book will help you move along that path, to impact, in a positive way, your understanding of and commitment to racial justice. At the end of the day, there is no way any of us Old White Dudes will ever fully *get it* regarding what it means to be Black in America. But that does not mean we don't have a responsibility to make the effort to better understand it. But more important, to do something . . . anything . . . large or small . . . to *make it* right, and move the needle forward.

Despite contrary claims, I believe we Old White Dudes have the capacity to understand, evolve, and do what is needed to meet that challenge.

We can do this!

# CHAPTER ONE

# A JOURNEY BEGINS

*"Success is a journey, not a destination. The doing is often more important than the outcome."*

—Arthur Ashe

**M**y first exposure to anything to do with Black Americans' struggle for justice occurred in 1967. I was ten years old, and Newark, NJ, a mere twenty miles from my hometown of Little Falls, was aflame with civil unrest. Newark was one of 159 US cities that erupted in rioting during what was dubbed the "Long Hot Summer of 1967."

Until then, my exposure to and awareness of people of color was limited to sports. Many of my sports heroes, Spider Lockhart and Homer Jones of the NY Giants, Willis Reed, Em Bryant and Bob Boozer of the NY Knicks, and Al Downing and Elston Howard of the New York Yankees, were Black.

The reverberations of the Newark unrest seeped through our lily-White town. I remember asking my parents about it. Their response was straightforward. Black people were protesting to achieve equal rights, which they deserved, and we supported. While I didn't fully understand or appreciate the issue at the time, it satisfied my ten-year-old mind. I went about my business of being a kid in my White town, White school, and White neighborhood. Like many ten- year-olds, I was in my own little world.

While issues of race weren't discussed regularly in our household, my parents made it clear that racism and intolerance would not be tolerated. For example, as a football coach, my father was clear about how coaches play the best players, regardless of color. But the most influential person in my life regarding issues of intolerance, empathy, and racism was my mother. While small in stature (her nickname was Pee Wee), she was a force of nature. She believed strongly in the humanity and basic decency of every human being. She didn't simply talk about it. She lived it through her volunteer work, particularly at a soup kitchen where she worked on a regular basis for as long as I can remember. She also demonstrated it in her everyday life. I cannot begin to tally the number of times she would stop to spend time with folks of any color or background. She had a natural inclination to connect with anyone and everyone. She was generous with compliments and encouragement and always found a way to make people of all walks of life smile. She made it crystal clear that everyone—without exception—is important and had a story to tell. She often reminded us that the true mark of character is reflected in how you treat the least fortunate among us and that every human being, regardless of race or station in life, deserved respect.

## HOMETOWN HOOPS

Those values formed the foundation for my real education about race when I fell in love with basketball. I was obsessed with the game. I would shovel snow from the local playground or at the hoop behind the town's police station to practice. I'd dribble my basketball while delivering newspapers on a route that conveniently ended within a block of my favorite courts. While I also played football and baseball and, largely due to my size, played them well, by the seventh grade I left those sports behind. Basketball would be it for me.

There weren't too many days when I played fewer than five or six hours. I'd arrive at school early to play before classes began and picked it up again at lunchtime. After school, I'd rush home to do my paper route (dribbling my basketball along the way), and when done, play until dinner. After dinner, I'd return to the lighted police station court and play until my nighttime curfew. Summers meant basketball camps and pickup games all day, every day. I couldn't get enough.

My earliest recollection of sustained interaction with people of color was through pick-up games. Back then, street basketball was thriving. Groups of players, young and old, rode all over Northern NJ in search of competitive games. We regularly went into Paterson, a struggling industrial city, looking for games where most players were Black or Hispanic/Latino. They returned the favor, traveling to our "home court" to play.

The time and effort paid off. I became quite good for my age. I was bigger and stronger than everyone in my class, and had shaped my skills by playing regularly against older and more talented players. At home, I constantly battled my two older brothers, both future college athletes, in all ways brothers compete. In high school, I started on the varsity team as a freshman in 1972 and set the New Jersey state scoring record for a freshman playing at the varsity level. That opened the door to various summer leagues, summer camps, and of course, continued pick-up games. The freshman scoring record helped spread my reputation, which in turn attracted players from around the area to the "cop station" to see what the fuss was about, to test this young White kid, to see if he was for real.

After a successful high school career, during which I scored over 2,500 points and received All-State honors, culminating with my jersey number being retired, I was highly recruited. I seriously considered Duke, Villanova, and Oregon, but chose Davidson College, located in the tiny, rural town of Davidson, NC, twenty miles north of Charlotte. I arrived the fall of 1975. My older brother Greg had also attended Davidson, playing both football and basketball, back when that sort of thing was possible.

## HOOPING IN A CHANGING LANDSCAPE

Davidson has a rich and storied basketball tradition. While most are familiar with Davidson's recent success during the Steph Curry years (2006–2009), Davidson was a perennial top-twenty team during the late 1960s and early 1970s. Along with five other freshman recruits, a recruiting class Davidson fans dubbed "The Super Six," I arrived on campus certain that the school's national success would continue. While things didn't quite turn out that way, my basketball experience at Davidson was, without a doubt, unique.

Little did I realize at the time that the college basketball world was in the middle of a seismic cultural and competitive shift. The driving force was race.

The first Black athlete to play at a predominately White school was William Henry Lewis at Amherst College, playing three seasons and serving as the team captain in 1891. While there were a few Black college athletes who followed (almost exclusively at Northern colleges), the first real drips of the integration of college basketball began in the late 1940s with Indiana's Bill Garrett in 1948. Teams at Southern schools were not integrated until the 1960s. For example, Mike Maloy, who led Davidson to national prominence, did not arrive on campus until 1966. The Southeastern Conference didn't integrate until 1966 when Perry Wallace arrived as a freshman at Vanderbilt University. Kentucky's Nate Worthington integrated SEC football in 1967.

The passing of the Civil Rights laws in the mid-1960s opened the doors of higher education to Black students. Of particular interest for coaches, athletic officials, and boosters was the opportunity to recruit Black athletes and, as a result, produce wins and put money in the bank. The floodgates had opened, and the number of Black athletes participating in college athletics skyrocketed.

While integration was positive, it created interesting challenges. The first related to academics. At the time, the academic standards to play (initial eligibility standards) and remain eligible to play (continuing eligibility standards) were virtually non-existent. Essentially, schools were allowed to set their own initial eligibility standards for incoming freshman. When it came to continuing eligibility, schools simply placed many of their athletes in "crib" courses and awarded them whatever grades they needed to remain eligible. Consequently, schools brought to campus an enormous number of athletes, especially in football and basketball, who were not prepared to succeed academically. Most were Black. This was a result of attending the segregated, underfunded schools of the Jim Crow era. And that many of these athletes were first generation college students further complicated the matter. The prospects of building a promising athletic program compelled coaches to recruit Black athletes on a full-scale, rush basis, regardless of their prospects for academic success. Far too many coaches cared about one thing and one thing only—how those athletes would advance their sports programs. Academic performance and graduation rates were secondary, at best.

Further complicating the dynamic was how to socially integrate Black athletes into a dominant White campus culture. One way to mitigate that challenge was, ironically, to further segregate them in athlete-exclusive dormitories. The result was the creation of a modern-day plantation system. Similar to how our nation's economic system was built with free labor in the form of enslaved Blacks, so too was the modern-day college athletic system built on the backs of free Black athlete labor. While some may claim that describing the system of major college athletics as a modern-day plantation system is hyperbole, it is not. That was the reality at the time and in some ways that same reality, while perhaps not as severe, still exists today.

When I arrived at Davidson, the college athletic world was in tremendous flux regarding integration. In Davidson's case, it was difficult to recruit Black athletes because of the dearth of Black students on campus. Additionally, unlike many other colleges and universities, Davidson did not bend academic standards to accept athletes who didn't have a reasonable chance to succeed academically and graduate. Thus, the pool of potential athletes from which Davidson could recruit was limited compared to most of our competitors.

During my freshman year, playing almost exclusively with freshmen, we won only five games. After the season, the school fired our coach and four of my five freshman teammates transferred. It descended from there. Over the course of my four-year career, we had five different head coaches, which must be an NCAA record. This included one coach who lasted a week and another who had a breakdown and left the team in mid-season. Almost twenty different assistant coaches and a boatload of players came and went. A once proud and nationally competitive program had devolved into utter disarray. Regardless, I persevered, finishing my career as the school's all-time leading scorer with almost 2,500 points and achieving All-American honors.

While my high school and college teams were predominantly White, between summer leagues, pick-up games, all-star games, and training camps, I spent plenty of time on teams that were predominantly Black. One memorable educational experience I had was as a member of a USA Basketball team that trained for two weeks in Cincinnati and embarked on a three-week foreign tour to several countries, including France, Israel, the USSR, and Yugoslavia. Traveling throughout Europe and behind the Iron Curtain as one of only three White players was a post graduate education in navigating an environment where I had little part in establishing the rules of engagement among the players. It was a significant life experience.

## PAY FOR PLAY

In 1979, I was a third-round draft pick of the New Jersey Nets. It wasn't the best time to attempt to make an NBA roster, particularly for a guy like me. While I had a good college career, I had no delusions about my chances. I didn't play for a big-name college powerhouse or for coaches who had strong NBA contacts. I was one of those players who needed to be selected by the right team, with the right system, and with some roster spots available for players without guaranteed contracts. While I was confident that I had the ability to play at the NBA level, I knew I needed some breaks to make it.

It was also a time when the NBA was in serious financial trouble. Consider that the 1979 NBA Finals were televised, not during prime time and not always live. Rather, games were aired at 11:30 PM and many on tape delay. It was widely perceived that the viewing public were so anemic about the league because it featured too many Black players, which, for too many Whites, conjured up images of a bunch of thugs, brandishing gold chains, making too much money, and doing drugs. Arenas were hardly full. Average attendance at NBA games during the 1978-79 season was 10,822 versus 2018-19 when it was 17,742. The league's television contract at the time was paltry relative to today's contracts. The result was a shaky financial foundation, which reduced rosters from twelve to eleven to cut costs. For my part, the Nets had eleven guaranteed contracts, which meant I had my work cut out for me.

I survived camp until the final cut and ended up playing a season with the Maine Lumberjacks in the Continental Basketball Association. The CBA was akin to baseball's minor league system and today's NBA G-League. It was where players, mostly final cuts from NBA rosters, landed to play to keep the promise alive of getting called up to the NBA if a roster spot opened. I was one of three White guys on a team of twelve players. Some players came and went, and so the roster fluctuated throughout the year. To say the environment around the Lumberjacks was different from my experience at Davidson would be a gross understatement.

At Davidson, everyone on the team was expected to graduate. Of the fifteen players who cycled through the Lumberjacks that season, only two or three of us had college degrees. It was an interesting cast of characters and made for an interesting and sometimes wild, year. While I broke a bone in my foot seventeen games into the season, I remained with the team to rehab. I'm glad of that because I saw, experienced, and learned a lot.

To be clear, I use this example of being a "minority" in the basketball world not to suggest that I have ever been the *victim* of racism in any way. Some folks refer to that as "reverse racism." I never experienced that in any significant way. My limited experience in facing the challenges of navigating a culture and environment in which I did not establish the rules and terms of engagement is, compared to Black

Americans, infinitesimal. Once practices or games ended, I returned to a White culture dominated world. That said, I did experience a small slice of being in the minority in a group, which left a strong and lasting impression and helped shape my world view around issues of race.

As mentioned, most of my teammates finished their eligibility and college careers without earning degrees. That got me thinking about the exploitation of major college athletes, particularly in football and basketball, which had a large percentage of Black athletes. It became obvious to me that far too many colleges and universities did not care about or feel any genuine sense of responsibility to meet their end of the deal they struck with scholarship players. The terms were simple: In exchange for an athlete's talents, the university would provide a legitimate opportunity to earn a meaningful athletic, academic, and social experience. Athletes have been meeting their end of the bargain for decades. Stadiums are full, television contracts are signed, and revenues are flowing.

The problem, however, was that universities were not meeting their end of the bargain. Yes, things have improved somewhat since the 1970s. But the fact remains; college athletics has a long and shameful history of exploiting basketball and football athletes, not only for university economic gain but also for personal gain in the form of massive salaries for coaches and administrators. From admitting academically unqualified athletes and demanding they spend over forty hours per week in athletically related activities, to placing them in crip courses geared to keep them eligible to play rather than on track to earn meaningful credits and a legitimate degree to cutting their scholarships due to injury, the system can be (and has been) exploitative. If schools conveyed an overriding message to athletes, it was this: "Just play ball and we will take care of everything else." Of course, why would this be a surprise? Given the history of our separate and entirely unequal K-12 educational system, why would the continued systemic denial of equal educational access, and an indifference to the quality of education Blacks receive be any different for Black college athletes?

Such institutional neglect and disregard for providing a well-balanced experience and education for athletes surfaced in interesting ways. For example, during my year in Bangor, Maine, after receiving our paychecks, a teammate asked for a ride to the bank. When I instructed the bank teller to deposit my check into my checking account, with some cash back, my teammate looked at me curiously and said, "What was that checking account thing about?" I explained that if you deposit money into the bank in either a checking or savings account, you can take that money back out of your account later. Here was a young person, a first-generation college student from an impoverished background, who had contributed to a college program for four years. You would have thought that a coach, athletic administer, or faculty member—someone, anyone—realizing he had a chance to make a good deal of money as a pro would have schooled him on at least the basics of personal finance. Of all the lessons I learned during my year in Bangor, that was the most illuminating.

The summer following my stint with the Lumberjacks, I had a tryout with the Golden State Warriors. Unfortunately, midway through mini-camp I badly sprained my ankle and did not get invited back to regular fall camp. While sorely disappointed, I couldn't help but think that somebody was trying to tell me something. Maybe it was time to move on to the next phase of my life.

When a dream ends, it can be a cold, harsh slap in the face. Athletic fame is fleeting. I was reminded of that in a humorous way when, a year after I had "retired," I was at a wedding of a Davidson teammate in Charlotte. The wedding occurred less than a mile from the Charlotte Coliseum, the site of most of our home games. Per wedding protocol, I was escorting family members and guests to their proper seats. A friend of mine was sitting in the back row behind an elderly couple and overheard the following exchange. The woman pointed at me and asked the man next to her, "Who is that really tall guy?" The man replied, "Oh, him? That used to be John Gerdy." Apparently, once I was no longer pursuing a basketball career, I wasn't even John Gerdy anymore.

Talk about a tough crowd!

Despite that, I had a great run and have no regrets. Basketball enabled me to earn a quality educational experience, represent the United States on the international stage, experience the life of a professional athlete, and meet tremendous people who opened many doors of opportunity. None of that would have happened without basketball. In that sense, I had a successful career in using the sport as a means to an end as opposed to an end in itself. Ultimately you, and you alone, get to define your personal success. That said, it was time to move on.

The disappointment of not playing in the NBA stung. But it also provided an opportunity to reinvent myself. Difficult experiences and disappointing events are not simply challenging; they also offer the opportunity to use hard-earned lessons as building blocks to take advantage of future opportunities. Generally, when one door of opportunity closes, if you keep your head up, eyes open, and do the necessary work, a different door of opportunity opens. The question is whether you are prepared to walk through that door.

# CHAPTER TWO

## CONTINUING EDUCATION

*"Education's purpose is to replace an empty mind with an open one."*
—Malcolm Forbes

From Bangor, I returned to Charlotte and took a job as the youth program director at the Johnston YMCA. The North Charlotte community we served was racially diverse and struggling economically.

Like many YMCAs, the Johnston Y served as the local community center where the neighborhood kids spent a lot of time simply hanging out. I loved that part of my job because kids are so honest and wide open in expressing their feelings and realities. It gave me a good view of the lives they and their families lived, and challenges they faced. It was every bit as enlightening as the education I received at Davidson and with the Maine Lumberjacks.

While my work during my two-year stay at the Y was rewarding, it became clear that college athletics would be a more effective tool and offered a larger platform to advocate for education. For me, athletics was never really about sports. It was about education and leveraging lessons learned on the courts and fields and applying them in life, using sports not as an end but a means to achieve success in life. The combination of a well-balanced athletic, social, and academic experience can be powerful and life changing. College athletics, particularly Division I athletics, allowed a bigger, more visible, and influential platform to advance those values. I came by this belief honestly because my parents made clear that academics always took precedence over athletics. If we did not perform academically, we wouldn't be allowed to perform athletically. Period.

I wanted to devote my life to that principle on a larger scale. In that sense, my apple didn't fall far from my parent's tree.

But how to do that? What would be next?

The answer was in Athens, Ohio.

## COLLEGE OF A DIFFERENT SORT

Tucked into Southeastern Ohio, not far from West Virginia, and well within Appalachia, Athens, Ohio, was the home of Ohio University (OU). Athens is one of the funkiest, most interesting, and below the radar screen hip towns in the US. Much to my surprise and delight, it became my home for the next four years. While a significant slice of the 18,000 students were from Ohio, there were large chunks from New York, New Jersey, Pennsylvania, and points beyond.

Most interesting about the OU student population was its mix of international students. OU has a strong program in International Studies that attracts students from all over the world. Athens was a blend of "townies," farmers, hippies, country folk from the hills of Appalachia, college faculty, undergraduates, and international students. Put them together and you had a spicey Appalachian gumbo tucked in an isolated and remote location far removed from the rest of the world.

OU was the first university in the nation to develop a master's program for sports administration professionals. To this day, it remains one of the nation's best. I was accepted and began to work toward a career in college athletics. After completing my master's, I remained at OU to pursue a doctorate in higher education. My goal was to become a Division I athletic director.

While at OU, my love affair with the game of basketball continued unabated. Whenever I moved into a new town, after finding a place to live, my next priority was finding a noon hoops pick-up game. From the Charlotte YMCA to Grover Center at OU, to a recreation center in Kansas City, to the Birmingham, Alabama YMCA, to the 92nd Street Y in New York City, to a community center in Dayton, to Millersville University in Lancaster PA, I've played a lot of noon hoops.

I continued to play basketball until my mid-50s when my body no longer allowed it. When it gets to the point where every morning you must negotiate with your knees, ankles, back, and other body parts to gain their cooperation for the day, it's a sign you may want to find exercise activities more physically forgiving, such as yoga or swimming. But the body parts needed to play while at OU were still cooperating, and I took full advantage.

What fascinates me about pick-up games is that each game is different. Each time you take the court you must assess the other nine players and adjust your game accordingly. You must work with all types of people of all levels of ability. Basketball is a microcosm of life, wonderfully diverse and full of possibilities.

After four years in Athens, with my doctorate in hand, I was ready to move on to my next adventure.

## KANSAS CITY, HERE I COME!

After graduating from OU, I found myself driving to Kansas City with the entirety of my possessions packed into a Honda Civic. At the time, Kansas City was the headquarters of the National Collegiate Athletic Association (NCAA), which had hired me as a legislative assistant. It was the perfect entre into the college athletics enterprise during what became an important era for the organization. Because of growing public skepticism about what many saw as a corrupt system, the NCAA had begun dedicating resources to assist schools to improve rules compliance. The fundamental principle of compliance is simple—you follow the rules. As legislative assistants, we educated coaches and athletic department personnel about NCAA rules and regulations and helped them create internal systems of checks and balances to assure compliance.

By 1986, it was painfully clear that college athletics programs were not following the rules. Many were, quite simply, out of control. Recruiting rules were routinely broken and academic standards got watered down to where they were almost non-existent. As a result, college presidents started to exert greater influence over how their sports enterprises were run. Until then, athletic directors and power coaches ran the NCAA. The attitude of college presidents had been that athletics weren't central to the educational mission of the institution (which is true!), and as long as athletic department news stayed on sports pages—and didn't leak onto newspaper front pages—presidents didn't pay much attention. But when recruiting scandals and academic fraud cases commanded increased attention from not only the public and media, but also Congress, college presidents inserted themselves into the oversight and control of their athletic departments.

For me, the timing was ripe. My NCAA arrival roughly coincided with the emergence of the NCAA Presidents Commission, which focused on implementing measures to increase institutional control and academic integrity. The emerging compliance movement squared with my fundamental philosophical beliefs regarding the proper role of athletics on campus. It was interesting and gratifying work. I felt that I was helping schools get more into line with the stated educational mission of college athletics.

It also gave me an unvarnished look into how badly college athletes, particularly in the sports of football and basketball, were exploited. Graduation rates were abysmal. While I had an immersive experience regarding the impact of that system while a Maine Lumberjack, my NCAA experience opened me to a more nationally ingrained problem, reinforcing what I had learned before. The longer I was exposed to the machinations and policies of the NCAA, the clearer it became that, at its core, major college athletics had little to do with education and more to do with generating enormous sums of money on the backs of football and basketball players, most of whom were Black. My world view and philosophy regarding college athletics and its impact on the Black athlete was evolving. I became more vocal about "student-athlete welfare." Yet, when push came to shove, I could see that few coaches or people in the athletic establishment advocated for the athletes.

For example, coaches and administrators had sports agents looking after their interests while NCAA rules prohibited athletes from similar representation. Compounding the problem was that athletes come and go. At most, they are on campus five years, and some are one-and-done. That fluidity limited opportunities to build effective advocacy structures to protect their rights and interests. As a former college athlete, I took it upon myself to advocate on behalf of the athletes, particularly as it applied to their academic and social welfare. I had seen, firsthand, how the system had failed so many of my former teammates and wanted to do something to draw attention to the deficiencies of that system.

After three years, I had become restless and was looking for another challenge. I wanted to find an opportunity to apply my beliefs, ideas, and world view in a more targeted fashion in the hope of having a more direct impact on athletes. While I enjoyed working on these issues on the national level at the NCAA, I determined that the best way to have a more direct impact would be to work for an athletic conference or an individual school. To that end, I accepted a job that would put me into the Belly of the Beast—the Southeastern Conference. In the fall of 1989, I again loaded up my Honda Civic and headed to Birmingham, Alabama to begin a new adventure as associate commissioner for compliance and academic affairs.

## INTO THE BELLY OF THE BEAST

To say that the Southeastern Conference (SEC) and I were an odd match would be an understatement. At the time, the widespread perception, much of it deserved, was that the two most out of control athletic conferences were the SEC and the Southwest Conference (which was dissolved in 1996), particularly regarding their football and men's basketball programs. It's also fair to say that the majority of Division I athletic cultures, particularly those with powerful football and basketball programs were, to varying degrees, out of control. Player payments, academic fraud, various recruiting violations, and schemes were commonplace, as were the many NCAA probations that resulted. It was not uncommon during this era to find half of the schools in the SEC or SWC on NCAA probation or under investigation at the same time.

I had two areas of responsibility at the SEC—compliance (you've got to play by the rules) and academic affairs (these kids are not pieces of meat and deserve a legitimate chance to earn a meaningful, well-balanced academic, athletic, and social experience). It was a wonderful opportunity, and I dove in headfirst.

The challenge, however, was that many administrators and coaches did not rejoice when informed of the changing expectations and responsibilities in the areas of compliance, academic integrity, and athlete welfare. My stance placed me at odds with the behavior I was expected to help change. I was an agent of change in a deeply entrenched and highly resistant culture. And it didn't help that I was a Yankee from New Jersey. Nor did it help that I was an ex-NCAA guy (not to be trusted because the NCAA investigates us and puts us on probation). And I had a PhD. In the big-time college athletic setting, "pointy-headed academic types" were often looked on a bit suspiciously. Finally, I was a basketball guy—not a football guy. So, there I was, a Yankee with a PhD who had worked at the NCAA and hadn't played football, challenging how things had been done for time eternal in the football-obsessed Southeastern Conference.

I hit an early speed bump. Shortly after accepting the job, the commissioner who had hired me, Harvey Schiller, asked that I outline my plans for implementing a comprehensive, conference-wide compliance program at a meeting of the SEC athletic directors. Great start I thought. As fate would have it, however, a few weeks before I was to present my plans, Schiller resigned to become executive director of the US Olympic Committee. I had lost the major inside support I had and was deeply concerned about presenting contentious matters without the presence and support of the league commissioner. I was flying solo in front of athletic directors and their staff in a league where football was religion and coaches and athletic directors were regional icons. With a few exceptions, I faced a table full of good ol' Southern boys whose priorities were clear—God, motherhood, apple pie, and football, and not necessarily in that order.

Idealistic and naïve, I gave them my best sales pitch about the importance of compliance, academics, institutional integrity, and student-athlete welfare. I told them how, with their help, we would turn the Southeastern Conference into a model of institutional control of athletics. When finished, the response was deafening.

Prolonged silence.

Finally, a long-time administrator leaned over the table, cleared his throat, slowly turned to me, and said, "Son, I don't know who you are or where you're from, but you best remember, you in the SEC now."

What had I gotten myself into?

That said, I also came to find that, for every "good ol' boy" in college athletics resistant to change no matter the price, there were others who wanted to do the right thing. Regardless, that meeting was a sobering welcome to the reality of the league and the hurdles ahead.

The SEC annual meeting was more of the same. Each spring, the league convened its annual meeting in Destin, Florida. The purpose of the gathering was to bring the members of the SEC "family" together to celebrate the end of the academic year and review conference and NCAA policies, issues, and proposals.

The legislative agenda included a series of measures designed to improve athlete welfare. These measures were in response to an NCAA sponsored survey that revealed how athletes were ill prepared and underperforming academically, and spending inordinate amounts of time on athletics. The athletes felt isolated from the general student body, and had scant financial resources and time to enjoy a well-balanced college experience. Among the measures was a proposal to address the feelings of isolation—the elimination of athletic dormitories.

By 1990, only a handful of schools housed athletes in "athlete only" dorms. Most were in the SEC. Having toured those dormitories during my first year in the league, I understood why athletes felt isolated. The dorms, while upscale compared with other dormitories, were usually located apart from other dorms and close to the athletic complex. And with "athlete only" cafeterias located in the same building, and the excessive athletically related time demands (averaging over forty hours per week) placed on athletes, the sense of separation and alienation from the general campus community was palpable.

The NCAA proposal to eliminate athletic dorms was designed to promote the integration of athletes into the campus community. National sentiment to eliminate the dorms was overwhelming, not only because there were so few remaining but, more important, the athletic dorm represented what many believed was most wrong about major college athletics. The symbolism of "penning up" mercenary athletes, most of them Black, for purposes of monitoring them virtually twenty-four hours a day to maximize their athletic performance, was damning.

The SEC meetings were structured to allow representatives from each school to meet with their peers. Athletics directors, faculty athletics representatives, senior women's administrators, and presidents met separately to discuss issues for which they were responsible. Also in attendance were head football coaches as well as the head men's and women's basketball coaches. Each group's agenda included a review of NCAA legislative proposals. Roy Kramer, the newly hired SEC commissioner, scheduled time to meet with each group to discuss the proposals. I was included in those meetings because of my knowledge of the rules and legislative process.

Given the size of the egos of most SEC football coaches, it was a miracle there was enough room for us to fit inside the conference room. In the Deep South, football coaches are second only to God, and perhaps the late Dale Earnhardt, as worship-worthy deities.

Kramer's introduction and explanation of the NCAA's proposed ban on athletic dorms ignited an inflammatory debate. The coaches were livid. This, they fumed, was something the SEC simply could not allow. No one, not even the NCAA, could tell them what was best for "their" players and "their" programs. The last straw occurred when Kramer tried to explain that, despite what they thought, the measure would pass overwhelmingly, and that, when it came to athletic dorms at least, they should accept that the SEC was the last of a dying breed.

The coaches weren't having it. Leaning out over the table, one coach turned to a rival coach of a school from the same state and drawled, "Coach, do you think we could get the state legislature to pass a law that would require all of our football players to live in athletic dorms?"

"I think we could do that," was the reply.

The coach then turned back to Kramer and sneered, "What do you think of *that*, Mr. Commissioner?"

This was but one example of how out of control major college athletics had become. It also personified the tremendous hubris of not only football coaches, but of the athletics enterprise as a whole. That arrogance continues today, exemplified by the words of legendary Alabama coach Paul "Bear" Bryant: "Fifty thousand people don't come to campus to watch an English class." Far too many coaches and athletics administrators continue to believe that athletics is bigger, better, and more important than the institution.

Housing athletes in separate dormitories represented the absolute worst in college athletics, treating athletes as cogs in a machine, isolated from the campus community to keep them focused on playing ball. That these dorms were used primarily for football and basketball teams, most members who were Black, on overwhelmingly white campuses, highlighted the "plantation mentality" that permeated many of these programs. On those campuses, football and basketball programs had little to do with education and their athletics departments were completely divorced from the academic community. The athletic dorm was the most glaring symbol of that reality.

The story of athletic dorms in the SEC provides an example of how things can change. The NCAA voted overwhelmingly to eliminate them. The sneering coach who had threatened to involve the state legislature was later forced to resign due to a series of NCAA violations. With state and national legislators, as well as the public, becoming increasingly skeptical of the growing commercialization and professionalization of college athletics, it is hard to imagine any state legislature bending to the will of a college football or basketball coach today, even in the SEC.

Fortunately, the increased pressure from college presidents to reform the enterprise and re-establish effective institutional control over their programs provided opportunities to implement compliance and academic support programs. For example, I now marvel that I convinced league leadership to allow a full day diversity training session at each school. It made perfect sense, at least to me. While most football and basketball athletes are Black—and in contrast the vast majority of the coaching staffs and administrators are White, the student bodies and people who filled the stands are overwhelmingly White, and the revenues generated to support athletic programs, including the non-revenue sports (such as the predominately White tennis, golf, and swimming programs), were funded off the virtually unpaid labor of Black athletes.

It is important to keep in mind, too, that each athletic program operation is overseen by a coach with enormous, unquestioned power and influence over "his" players. From my perspective, as far as a power construct in concerned, it is not all that different from the old "plantation bosses" during slavery. Is that hyperbole? I don't think so. Coaches had complete, absolute, and unquestioned power over their players, who were, in essence, "workers" who generated a very lucrative entertainment *product.*

Of course, the question is how they wielded that absolute control and authority. Some did it with a measure of empathy and commitment to the general welfare of the players in their charge. But many others didn't care about any of that. To them, college football and basketball were cold, hard, win-at-any-cost businesses, and the players represented "assets" they could leverage to the greatest extent possible to win games and produce revenue and glory for themselves and the institution.

But much to my surprise and delight, after a long, diligent campaign, the university presidents signed off on the program, allowing the Anti-Defamation League to conduct diversity training to raise and discuss issues around athlete welfare and athletic department culture. After I informed a fellow compliance officer from another conference that I intended to push the program through the SEC, he shook his head and replied, "Diversity training in the SEC? Good luck with that! In the meantime, you might want to update your resume."

Simply doing the research, legwork, and consensus building required to get the program approved created angst and resistance from some quarters. Some groups, such as the Faculty Athletic Representatives and Academic Counselors, supported the idea. Others, mostly coaches, were not happy with me. They didn't appreciate a Yankee bringing a New York civil rights organization to "educate" them regarding issues relating to discrimination and athlete rights. The implication was that their programs were racist. While I expected that reaction, I didn't expect what occurred within the first five minutes of the initial ADL session. The head football coach got up and said something like, "I don't know why we are here. We don't have a race problem in this athletic department. When I or any of these other coaches look at a player, we don't see color. We see an athlete. And whoever earns the right to play, gets to play."

As a coach, of course you don't see color when putting together your team. The only color that big time football and basketball coaches see is the color of money. They are fully aware that if they don't win, they will be fired. So, it would be idiotic not to play the best players, regardless of color.

But here's the question. Did they see color when recruiting athletes even though they were not prepared for college work? Did they see color when they were put into "crib" courses to keep them eligible? Did they see color when denying them a legitimate opportunity to earn a meaningful academic, athletic, and social experience? Did they see color when they viewed these athletes as slabs of meat, whose primary purpose was to perform athletically, win games, and generate revenue? Did they see color when they communicated with them, and in how they treated them? And how much time did they earnestly devote to helping them navigate their lives off the fields and courts?

Many say that without sports and the opportunity athletic programs provide, these athletes would never be able to better their lot in life. That said, I was beginning to wonder if, in fact, many of them were better off. For example, were they better off when they used up their eligibility without earning a degree? Or when an athlete sustained a career-ending injury and was cut loose by the program because they were no longer productive? Or, when they were unceremoniously kicked off the team and their scholarship revoked for the rather vague term, "violation of team rules?" Given that so many of these athletes were Black, often poor and many first-generation college students, they were "disposable" in the eyes of far too many coaches. From my viewpoint, it seemed that an athletic department's mindset and narrative was that those who did not "make it" were bad apples, lazy or flawed in some way. In other words, when kids didn't "make it," it was the kid's fault. But for those kids who did graduate and "make it," the athletic department and coaches were first in line to claim it was the system and their coaching and mentorship that molded these athletes into successful adults.

Obviously, a lack of self-awareness regarding the possibility that in some cases, the system may have failed the kid allowed athletic department personnel to convince themselves they had no responsibility for preparing these young people for a productive life after their playing days. There were certainly cases where a particular kid may have been a bad apple, but from my vantage point, the system was wildly stacked against them as far as their right to a legitimate opportunity to earn a quality educational and social collegiate experience. In short, far too often it was made clear in ways large and small that athletes were on campus first and foremost to play ball.

After six years of poking and prodding the SEC on issues relating to compliance, student-athlete welfare, and academic integrity, I was beginning to wear out my welcome as there were more than a few people in the league who fought those changes in ways large and small. I can't tell you how many times a coach or administrator would accuse me of being "out to destroy college athletics." Nothing was further from the truth. I was trying to hold our schools accountable for acting in conformity with their avowed primary purpose—to provide an honest and legitimate chance for their athletes to earn a meaningful academic, social, and athletic experience. In other words, to do what college athletics claims to do and be about.

It was an interesting six years. And we did make some progress. The SEC was the first conference to establish a Student-Athlete Advisory committee as well as a new coach's orientation program where issues related to compliance, student welfare, and academic integrity were highlighted and discussed. We also instituted various measures to increase oversight and accountability of coaches and staff as it related to rules and regulations.

Regardless, it was time to move on, but I did so with mixed feelings. I truly enjoyed my time in Birmingham. Despite its checkered civil rights history, there was a side of the city I loved. A large part of that was because I had an interesting "double agent" life there. By day, I was Dr. John Gerdy, a buttoned down, conservative, SEC executive. By night, however, I was known around the Five Points section of town as a blues musician named Willie Marble. This is my stage name and performance persona; an old-time, old school (usually in jacket with white shirt and tie) blues man.

It's a lot of fun to have a stage name and an alter ego. I'd highly recommend it. Although, I tell my friends that if I adopt another three or four alternative personas, get me some professional help . . . quickly. Why the Delta Blues? That's simply the genre of music to which I have always gravitated. When I play and sing, it's simply what comes out. I'd best be described as a blues "shouter," a performer whose "singing" is less singing than it is shouting. My favorite musician, Howlin' Wolf, was a blues shouter. There's nothing contrived about my blues persona. Some may disagree and call my performing and adopting a blues persona "cultural appropriation" and that I am disrespecting Black culture. To the contrary, my intention is to honor, celebrate, and spread the word about that heritage. In other words, it's not about appropriation but rather "appreciation." Most important, it's what's in my soul. It's what I feel and it's what comes out when I open my mouth to sing. While I respect and honor the fact that the blues derived from Black culture, the fact is, the blues as an art form is universal.

While I felt that I had taken my reform efforts at the SEC about as far as I could have, the other deciding factor in my decision to move on was that it seemed as if I was beginning to spend more time being Willie Marble than John Gerdy. When that happens, it's a clear sign that it's time to get out of town.

# CHAPTER THREE

# PASSIONS RECOGNIZED AND ACTED UPON

*"Conceive, believe and achieve."*

—Lailah Gifty Akita

Our first child, Emily Wallace Gerdy, was born on January 13, 1995, and her timing couldn't have been better. Her birth, combined with the fact that my wife had a high pressure, extremely demanding corporate job, provided an opportunity to leave the SEC and reinvent myself as a stay-at-home dad. It is an experience I wouldn't trade for anything. I thoroughly enjoyed my new life.

In addition to my days being filled with childcare responsibilities, which doubled when James was born in 1997, I was also afforded the opportunity to begin to write about my experiences and philosophies regarding college athletics and higher education reform and the role of athletics in our schools and culture. From 1997 – 2006, I published four books, *The Successful College Athletic Program: The New Standard* (1997), *Sports in School: The Future of an Institution* (2000), *Sports: The All-American Addiction* (2002), and *Air Ball: American Education's Failed Experiment with Elite Athletics* (2006) as well as many essays in journals, newspapers, and magazines. A central theme throughout my writing has been the issue of the economic and educational exploitation of college athletes, particularly in the sports of football and basketball.

In short, I have been observing, contemplating, and writing about these issues for a long time. That's because I believe strongly that sports can be a powerful educational and community building tool as well as a powerful example for social change. The fundamental principles that drive progress in these areas are fairness, tolerance, cooperation, and equal opportunity. Sports is a wonderfully effective platform through which these principles can be demonstrated.

By 2005, the kids were getting older. That meant they did not need dad around as much. I began thinking about what was next. How could I, once again, reinvent myself? My initial inclination was to find something in college athletics. Upon further consideration, I concluded, "Been there, done that." The other driving factor was that I had become disillusioned regarding the direction of major college athletics. It was becoming increasingly less aligned with my beliefs regarding academic integrity and student-athlete welfare. I was no longer willing to defend and justify the hypocrisy of the industry's claims to be, first and foremost, "about education." It was time for something new.

But what?

I decided to pursue a path that combined two of my life passions—education and music. My thought was to apply my knowledge, skills, resources, and passion to form an organization to promote school music programs. In researching the lay of the land, two trends became clear. First, music programs were being cut dramatically, particularly in underserved school districts, mostly due to an increased emphasis on student math, reading, and science test scores, which had become vital to securing state education funding.

And second, these cuts were being made despite a growing mountain of research showing that music programs are a highly effective educational tool. This wasn't surprising as music is math. Music is reading. Music is logic. Music is science. It is truly the universal language.

Perhaps most important, music nurtures and develops creativity and collaborative skills. The ability to think creatively and "out of the box" to solve problems as well as being able to collaborate with others are two vital characteristics business leaders seek in their employees and citizens expect of their leaders and public servants. Like team sports, involvement in a band, choral group, or orchestra teach the same important collaborative skills and instill vital character traits. I've been both on a five-person basketball team and in a five-person band. The skills required for success and the lessons learned are identical.

Further, every challenge we face, whether as a city, state, nation, or global community, from healthcare, to the environment, to civil rights, to global politics in this fast paced, increasingly diverse, and interconnected world, is becoming more complex. And the only way we are going to be able to solve those increasingly complex issues is to develop in our populace, a corresponding increase in creativity and the ability to think outside the box. Nothing in our educational arsenal teaches creativity more effectively than music and the arts.

Despite that fact, there is an ongoing debate within education circles regarding whether music is a core subject, a co-curricular activity, or an extracurricular activity. A more accurate description of music's educational effectiveness is that because of its universal nature, it is the glue that holds the entire curriculum together. It is critical, fundamental subject matter. Relying on this perspective, in 2006, a group of friends and I founded Music For Everyone (MFE), a nonprofit Community Benefit Organization (CBO) in Lancaster County, PA, with a mission to cultivate the power of music as an educational and community building tool.

In 2006, we conducted our first fundraiser. We raised about $11,000, which we used to purchase instruments for the School District of Lancaster, a district where almost 95 percent of the students qualify for the federally funded school lunch program.

We were off and running.

## EXPANDING OUR MISSION AND IMPACT

After the initial grants, word spread about what we had done. We were striking a chord in the community. We conducted a few more fundraising events and purchased more instruments. MFE started to grow. What has been so exciting and gratifying regarding the evolution of MFE is how we've continued to expand the scope and reach of our programming. There are two reasons for this. First, we have a broad mission—to cultivate the power of music. And second, as noted, music is the universal language. As such, the potential to leverage its educational and community building benefits is virtually unlimited. That provides much room for flexibility in identifying and taking advantage of opportunities to grow and, as a result, expand our impact. Such flexibility for CBOs is vital in our increasingly complex, fast moving, and rapidly evolving culture and society.

That flexibility has allowed us to apply and leverage the organization's resources to begin to address a wide range of community issues and societal challenges far beyond our initial focus on music in the schools.

For example, we were also learning and experiencing music's tremendous power and potential to bring people together and build community.

Here's an example:

Each summer since 2010, MFE places between ten and twenty designed and painted pianos throughout downtown Lancaster. These pianos are available to the public to play 24/7 for four months throughout the summer. Whether a virtuoso performer or a beginner, whether you play chopsticks or Chopin, everyone has access to these pianos. One impact of Keys for the City is that everyone who has played one or heard one being played while walking through town is connected. They all share this common civic and public experience. Literally tens of thousands of magical musical moments occur around these pianos each summer with people of all ages, races, and beliefs coming together to share the magic and community building power of music.

But here is where Keys for the City goes beyond merely notes played and songs sung.

When we informed the city's mayor of our plan, he responded, "Have you guys lost your minds? They won't last a week before they are vandalized." To his credit, he followed with, "It's a crazy idea, but let us know what we can do to help." While we recognized the risk, we offered a different public narrative. We believed in Lancaster's better angels. We believed that our community would embrace, enjoy, and take care of the pianos. And, true to form, Lancastrians disproved the naysayers. After twenty pianos were on the streets available 24/7 for four months, there was but one vandalism incident. This public display of caring has resonated throughout our community. It has instilled a sense of pride in the decency and integrity of the citizens of Lancaster. Keys for the City has had a profound impact on Lancaster's vibrant arts scene, bringing people together by providing the random gift of music all summer long. It is a powerful testament to music's tremendous community building potential. Keys has also contributed to Lancaster's efforts to brand the city as an arts community and destination to spur economic vitality and growth.

Several years ago, I started reading and doing research regarding a newly emerging health care tool—music therapy. Although, "newly emerging" is misleading because music has been used as a healing tool for as long as music has been played. For example, research shows that music can be effective in managing pain and treating dementia, PTSD, and depression, among a host of other health issues. Yet, despite that history and potential, until recently, it hadn't been widely embraced by the "traditional" medical community but was considered "alternative" in nature. This seemed like a great opportunity for MFE to see if we could, once again, leverage music's potential to impact our community in a positive manner.

Accordingly, in 2018, we launched a new initiative titled, "Music for Everyone's Well-Being," through which we award grants to organizations that use music as a healing tool. We're also exploring and developing programs and initiatives as well as helping to fund other public health initiatives and organizations that leverage music's healing powers. For example, we partner with an organization that uses poetry to help veterans suffering from PTSD. We provide musicians to work with the veterans to put their poems to music, culminating in an annual public performance on Veterans Day. Again, our ability to be lean, nimble, and flexible allows us to incorporate additional elements into our mission as new community needs emerge.

Which begs the question. Why is it that school and community music programs continue to be downsized or eliminated? The world is changing too rapidly for decision makers to continue to fund programs without considering changing educational, community and societal needs, challenges, and opportunities.

That rapidly changing environment has caused me to re-examine the relative return on investment of music versus athletics, in particular football. This was the major thrust of my fifth book, *Ball or Bands: Football vs. Music as an Educational and Community Investment*. In it, I provide a ROI analysis of the two activities. Several areas of impact were considered, including direct educational benefits in math, reading, language, logic, and creativity, various health impacts, including the development of the brain, impact on school culture, and influence on personal character development. After compiling and processing all that information, I concluded that if this were a football game, it'd be a rout: Music 55 and Football 20. In short, music's educational value, impact and return on educational investment, far outweighs that of football.

Many friends wondered why I changed my career focus from college athletics to music education and advocacy. For me, it made perfect sense. The two fundamental interests that have shaped my life are education and community service, both of which my parents hardwired into my DNA. Founding and serving as volunteer executive director of a non-profit organization focused on providing equal access to school and community music education programs and opportunities for children and adults primarily from underserved communities aligned perfectly with what was important to me. It was the ideal personal direction.

That said, we didn't have any idea what we were asking for when we created MFE in 2006, but what we got has been seventeen years of continued growth, an expanding mission, and increased community impact. MFE has invested over four million dollars in school and community music programs in the form of instrument grants, instruction, scholarships, and other program support. I've served as the full-time, non-salaried executive director from the beginning. That track record led to a decision to undertake what may be our most impactful initiative to date. It certainly has been the most difficult and risk filled. It is the subject of the following chapter, and will serve as the basis for much of the remaining narrative of this book—*Music For Everyone's Songs For Justice*.

# CHAPTER FOUR

## SONGS FOR JUSTICE

*"You can't help it. An artist's duty, as far as I am concerned,*
*is to reflect the times"*

—Nina Simone, American Singer-Songwriter

For my money, WBGO radio, which broadcasts from Newark, NJ, is the world's finest jazz station. Founded in 1979, WBGO bills itself as a publicly supported cultural institution that preserves and elevates America's music: jazz and blues.

Due to the wonders of the internet, you can live stream WBGO anywhere in the world. Case in point, I was at the Sun Gate at the end of the Inca Trail in Peru. Looking down upon Machu Picchu at an elevation of over 9,000 feet, a wild thought jumped into my high-altitude addled brain. *WBGO? Up here? Is that even possible?* I dialed it up on my iPhone and was soon listening to WBGO deep in the heart of the Andes mountains.

What an amazing world we live in!

As our tour group was ready to move on, I heard a snippet of an in-studio interview with a young jazz musician. I didn't catch his name, but heard him explain how artists are responsible to tell the stories of what goes on in our society and culture. "As an artist", he said, "it's part of the deal. You have a powerful platform. But you must wield that power thoughtfully and responsibly."

Music has always been a powerful platform to frame, highlight, generate debate, and spur change regarding issues relating to social justice. While we all have a responsibility to bear witness to events in the world around us, for musicians, artists, poets, and playwriters that responsibility is more fundamental. It is the essence of what they do. Music allows us to leverage our voices, like a mirror, creating a reflection of the world we live in.

John Lennon described it this way. "My role in society, or any artist's or poet's role, is to try to express what we all feel. Not to tell people how to feel. Not as a preacher. Not as a leader, but as a reflection of us all."

Or, in the words of Trent Reznor, founding member of Nine Inch Nails, "I have influence, and it's my job to call out whatever needs to be called out, because there are people who feel the same way but need someone to articulate it."

Sadly, athletes and artists continue to face blowback and criticism for using their platforms to raise our collective consciousness regarding timely and relevant issues. Far too many continue to believe athletes, artists, and musicians should just shut up and play, paint, or sing. In other words, they should simply entertain us and shouldn't comment on the important social, cultural, or political issues of the day. Really? You mean that athletes, musicians, and artists can't make their voices heard regarding issues that impact their lives and communities? To expect them not to speak out and bear witness to those issues misses the essence of being an artist, musician, or athlete.

Now more than ever, we need artists, athletes, and musicians to continue to reflect the times. As I heard at the Sun Gate, it's part of the deal. And when done thoughtfully and responsibly, we are all better for it.

Like my own reinvention opportunities, the civil unrest during summer 2020 provided an opportunity for MFE to reimagine its mission and programming in the context of current events. We have prided ourselves on being flexible, nimble, and lean with a capacity to pivot and utilize the power and potential of music to highlight and address emerging community challenges and needs. In today's rapidly changing world, you must be.

Songs For Justice (SFJ) was born out of the time-honored tradition of artists and musicians acting responsibly to *bear witness* to events transpiring around them. The spark that led MFE to undertake the SFJ project was the social unrest following the murder of George Floyd at the hands, or more accurately, under the knee of a Minneapolis police officer on May 25, 2020. Businesses and organizations, in response to the widespread civil unrest, were quick to write a social justice statement in support of the Black Lives Matter movement. While well-intentioned, most of what was written was simplistic and predictable. They said, in one form or another, the same three things:

"Black Lives Matter."

"We will do better on issues relating to justice and equity."

"We are all in this together."

A Black Lives Matter sign would then be posted in the window or front yard, and they washed their hands of the issue. "Whew! We're done with that. Now life can get back to normal."

It's not that easy.

While MFE published a thoughtful statement (included in Appendix B), the response felt hollow to us. We needed to do more than simply talk about it. We needed to act upon our convictions in a concrete way.

As a highly visible community benefit organization (CBO), we had a responsibility to do something real. Our responsibility was even greater because of the means (music) we employ for community impact. Music's power and potential as a social change agent has been a part of every social justice and human rights movement throughout history. We felt a responsibility to leverage that history and power. Equally important was that most of the people we serve are children and families of color. And, as a bonus, the proceeds we generate through sponsorships and donations are then invested in our schools to provide increased access to music education opportunities and programs for that population.

SFJ is a limited-edition series of vinyl records (45s) we release periodically. Each record features a specific racial, ethnic, or interest group (Black, Latino/Hispanic, LGBTQ+, women, refugees, and others) and addresses the challenges those groups face in today's world. Additionally, some records highlight and explore issues such as criminal justice reform. We called upon Lancaster musicians of all backgrounds to record songs about current issues of race, justice, and equity. We placed those songs on side A of the record. Side B includes either a historical speech on civil and human rights read by a local Lancaster personality or an original spoken word recording by a local artist.

For example, volume one featured a speech by abolitionist Thaddeus Stevens (who represented Lancaster in the US House of Representatives) read by Pedro Rivera, president of Thaddeus Stevens College of Technology. Volume two, which highlighted LGBTQ+ issues, featured a reading of the 2015 *Obergefell v Hodges* US Supreme Court decision affirming the constitutional right for same-sex couples to marry read by Marshall Snively, president of Lancaster City Alliance. Volume three featured an excerpt from Frederick Douglass's speech titled, *The Hypocrisy of American Slavery,* read by Ismail Smith-Wade-El, chair of Lancaster's City Council at the time who now represents Lancaster in the PA House of Representatives. The record is accompanied by a website that provides additional information and educational materials as well as digital downloads of the music.

Each record also includes a twelve-page insert booklet that includes visual art, poetry, graphic design, photography as well as historical analysis of pertinent issues, discussion questions, and inspiring quotes. SFJ is a multi-disciplinary platform that allows musicians, artists, and creatives of all types to bear witness to what is going on in the world around them. We have attempted to be strategic and directed in our efforts to identify and enlist contributors of all backgrounds and colors, all of them compensated. The result has been a virtual rainbow collection of diversity.

Finally, each record highlights a Lancaster-based nonprofit CBO doing affective work around justice and equity. Our aim is to provide these organizations a platform to tell their story to the public. We also provide them a hundred copies of the record to raise resources for their organization. It is a way to build synergies among CBOs around issues of justice and equity.

When you tally the various contributors over several records, it's a lot of people. Our efforts have not only yielded a virtual rainbow collection of diverse contributors, it's also a real-world testament to the power of diversity. While we still have much more work to do in leveraging SFJ, it is clearly meeting our goal of educating and spurring community debate and hopefully, inspiring people to act around these issues.

## THE POWER OF DIVERSITY

Whether as an individual, business, or CBO, it is important to periodically take an unvarnished look in the mirror. Such honest self-reflection can reveal uncomfortable truths about yourself or your organization. We do not do that often enough. It can be quite painful when, after such honest self-examination, you find you might not be living up to the standards and ideals you profess to believe in and act upon. Throughout the process of researching and writing this book, I have experienced those feelings, both personally and through MFE organizationally.

For example, we began a 360-degree review of our policies, procedures, and bylaws seeking to identify criteria and goals for strategically diversifying the organization. There is no question that these measures have made us a much better organization. But the fact is, we should have made these efforts long ago. While we have had POC on our board, we were not directional and strategic regarding our diversity efforts nor how that diversity could be leveraged to effectively advance our mission. Why didn't we? In a word, we (particularly me as executive director) were, quite frankly, lazy. I take full responsibility for that.

This is what I mean by lazy. Most children and families we serve are of color. While we may not have consciously thought this, I've come to realize that, subconsciously, we were using that as an excuse to not feel any sense of urgency to become more diverse organizationally. We used the makeup of our constituency as a *free pass* on having to make a serious, top-to-bottom, commitment to diversity. After much reflection, self-assessment, and critique, we have come to realize that precisely *because* we serve primarily children and families of color, our organization should reflect that diversity. By not doing so, we were underperforming because we didn't fully leverage our resources to best serve our main constituents and fundamental mission. This was a painful realization. How could we think we were serving a particular group to the best of the organization's ability if we did not have organizational representation of that group? How can an overwhelmingly White organization think they are most effectively serving a population consisting largely of POC without a strong presence of POC throughout the organization? While we are proud of the work we have done, I lament that we could have done more and done it more effectively had we been a more aware and diverse organization.

In short, the effect of SFJ on MFE has been transformational. In addition to finding that there are many practical organizational benefits that have accrued because of those efforts, we came to realize that embracing diversity is not only the right thing to do, but also the smart thing. While we quickly came to understand the impact of our efforts on MFE specifically, what has taken more time to come to light is how that impact has stretched beyond MFE to our city and community.

We have found that by providing a platform for a diverse cast of musicians, artists, poets, muralists, spoken word performers, and other creatives, who heretofore may not have had such a prominent platform, their visibility in our community has increased. By leveraging our high visibility as a CBO to offer opportunities for a more diverse group of creatives to *show their stuff*, their individual public platforms have expanded. Further, with that increased visibility and platform, their confidence, public reach, community networks, and opportunities also increased.

But here is the critical point.

It is safe to say that the benefits of our actions not only positively impacted MFE, but that positive impact also accrued to the city itself. To be clear, I am not implying that MFE has been solely responsible for leveraging the arts to spur community progress around DEI issues. It is not like there weren't other community organizations undertaking various efforts to leverage the impact of the arts for the same purposes. Organizations like the Lancaster County Community Foundation, South Central PaARTners, The Arts at Millersville University, The Mix, and the City of Lancaster itself, among other organizations, were also underwriting grants, initiating arts related programs, and leveraging their resources to achieve the same purposes. Rather, I make this point as a testament to the synergistic powers of the arts to transform communities. Given their universal nature, the arts, perhaps more than any other societal asset, have the power and potential to initiate such broad-based, community-wide change. But no group or organization can do this alone. To achieve meaningful change, it takes collaboration and a widespread community commitment, followed by strategic and directed action.

That said, we are already a better, stronger, and more effective organization because of the SFJ project. It's another example of how diversity equals strength.

Here's an example. One of my favorite MFE programs is our summer camp. Generally, we offer two-three weeks of camp, each hosting approximately one hundred children. I love this program so much that in 2019, I participated in the camp—as a camper. I was a member of the percussion section, along with four students, each no older than twelve. It was a blast!

The camp is free and open to anyone. Because of that, we attract kids of all backgrounds. The MFE faculty director is Dr. Michael Jamanis, a Julliard trained world class violinist. Several years ago, Michael began a career transformation as he was becoming less interested in the White dominated classical music industry, and thus began to explore a new musical direction. The timing was serendipitous as we were looking for someone to start our music education programming. He began going into schools and working alongside teachers and directly with students. He fell in love working with this diverse group of students, which led to the creation of our after-school strings program as well as our summer camp program. Along the way, he became increasingly interested in leveraging music as a tool to highlight and educate regarding issues relating to social justice.

As a result of his effort and leadership, we have built an MFE faculty, which at this writing includes two full-time and four part-time instructors, as well as several independent contractors and volunteers. Additionally, his interest in and commitment to using music as a tool to promote justice and equity continued to grow. To that end, he pushed us to join the El Sistema organization, a music education program founded in Venezuela in 1975 by Venezuela educator, musician, and activist Jose Antonio Abreu. A major focus of El Sistema is using music to promote social change. And, after the George Floyd murder, our relationship with El Sistema has taken on more urgency.

I witnessed the fruits of our efforts recently when attending the end-of-week summer camp concert. On stage the student makeup was extremely diverse with a mix of White, Asian, Hispanic, and Black youth. But just as important was the makeup of the faculty, half Black, and half White, which had previously been almost exclusively White. There's an enormous benefit to having teachers and role models who look like you. While we still have room to improve as it applies to perfectly reflecting the children we serve, this represents significant progress. Achieving that balance and diversity did not occur randomly. We had to make intentional and directed decisions that, over time, resulted in a more diverse faculty and organization. We threw out a seed, watered it, and, in time, it bore fruit.

Here's another example of how bringing more diversity into your organizational orbit reaps tremendous benefits. As mentioned, we've met and begun to work with many musicians, poets, spoken, word artists, and other creatives of color through SFJ who are also committed to using their art form, whether rap, hip hop, poetry, beats, photography, videography, or technology to educate and drive social change. These young creatives have been going into schools and community centers and leveraging the educational potential of their art forms to impact kids. The use of these genres, particularly rap, hip-hop, and beats clearly does not fall into the "traditional" educational material and model. It's a different medium. When I asked Terian Mack, whose essay appears later in this book, about this he explained, "Rap and hip-hop is the largest selling genre of music in the world. All these kids, regardless of color or background, are listening to it. To get their attention, you've got to meet them where they are."

Terian's lesson was fascinating and eye opening for me. And given one of MFE's primary functions is to provide music education instruction, it was something that we had to consider and pay attention to. For the most part, the instruction we had been offering was rooted in the White, Western classical model. That is certainly one avenue to teach music. However, by not considering, encouraging, and supporting these alternative approaches and the artists who employed them, we were limiting our reach and potential for educational impact. In response to that neglect, we have made an organizational commitment to helping to find ways to support these musicians, artists, and creatives in their efforts to leverage their art forms for positive educational and community impact, and to increase our effectiveness as an organization.

And in a nod to the potential of merging cross cultural art forms, Dr. Jamanis has not only begun implementing some of the elements of rap, hip-hop, and improvisation into his teaching curriculum, he has also been composing and performing with some of these rap and hip hop artists. The synergistic energy at the nexus of White, Western, classical, and urban, Black, hip-hop has been exciting, inspiring, and groundbreaking.

To reiterate, it's not enough to acknowledge the need to become more diverse. That is but the first step. Once acknowledged, the next step is to follow through with intentional and direct actions to achieve diversity. Becoming more diverse as an organization is not simply about adding a few POC to the board. Rather, it is evaluating all aspects of your programs, services, and structures from top to bottom. While change will not occur overnight, the fact is, it won't occur unless you as an individual or as an organization take directed, strategic actions, big and small, to embrace and leverage diversity and, as a result, become more effective in meeting your mission.

At the end of the day, while we still have much more work to do, the greatest lesson we have learned as an organization through the Songs for Justice project is that commitment to meaningful, genuine DEI is not about charity or burnishing public perception and reputation. It is about business and organizational effectiveness. In other words, embracing diversity is not only the right thing to do, but also the smart thing.

# CHAPTER FIVE

# BUMPS IN THE ROAD AND LESSONS LEARNED

*"We all require and want respect, man, or woman, Black or White. It's our basic human right."*

—Aretha Franklin

Developing and implementing SFJ has not been easy. That's not surprising given the subject matter. Issues around social justice and race are raw and are being played out against a public and cultural environment sitting on a knife's edge. SFJ has had its share of missteps and unexpected hurdles. While we realized the project would be extremely challenging, we also knew it provided many opportunities.

The first challenge involved efforts to assemble a team to get the project off the ground. SFJ is a big undertaking with many elements and moving parts. We needed a steering committee to establish and guide the general direction and execution of the program. Additionally, we needed a group to identify and recruit musicians, artists, poets, photographers, graphic-designers, and others to participate in the program. We did all this with the guiding principle that the project must reflect a broad and diverse group of participants. We were challenged to reach out and identify people and organizations with which we previously had little interaction. It stretched us. It forced us to rethink everything we did regarding diversity and inclusion.

That said, along the way, we encountered some significant bumps in the road. The first occurred as we were putting together the committees and identifying the creatives and vendors we would engage. I put together a list for presentation to the board. When we discussed the graphic designer we wanted to hire, a board member asked, "Have we bid this service out to the public? Have we considered a person of color for this job?" While the committees and personnel we had lined up to get the project off the ground was extremely diverse, we had not considered a POC for the graphic design function. We had simply plugged in the company we'd always used for our design work. It is a successful firm that has received multiple national awards for their work. They were instrumental in helping to establish our unique brand and *vibe*. Their work for us had been consistently excellent and they bill at below-market rate. They were an automatic choice.

The board pushed back and directed the staff to identify and interview a designer who was a POC before making a final decision. That threw us into a bit of a panic because we had deadlines looming. Further, we did not know of any locally owned design firms run by POC that could execute a project of this scope.

We put the project on pause while we identified potential local, minority-owned firms. As it turned out, there were not many. We identified a young designer who had a one-person shop, asked for and received a proposal, and interviewed him. It soon became clear that our longtime design firm was far better equipped to handle the project. That said, it was an interesting experience and process and, to be honest, an example of trying too hard to accommodate diversity. In short, we bent over backwards to make it work. You could sense that the committee was rooting for him. But it soon became clear that he was not the right fit for the project at that time. While virtually everyone agreed he underperformed during the interview, there were some committee members who wanted to give him the benefit of the doubt. The reasoning was that his youth and inexperience could be overcome with sufficient oversight and tutoring by the committee. In what was a surreal moment, the conversation shifted, and the group agreed to give him a chance, despite his poor showing.

I left the Zoom call, stunned with the decision, and agonized over how to approach the issue. It was clear to me that this was not a good decision for MFE. When hiring vendors, you do not expect, nor should you feel, that because of their youth and inexperience, you should have to mentor them. The expectation is that you are hiring a professional who does not need mentoring. It was not a learn-on-the-job project. The stakes were too high. I emailed the committee and asked for a few days to think about it and began talking through the issue with trusted and diverse advisors. I agonized over the decision, examining the ramifications from every angle. In the end, I made an executive decision not to hire him. As an executive director, you strive to honor decisions made by a committee. There are times however, when executive decisions must be made. After all the time, energy, resources, and emotion expended over sixteen years building MFE, I simply was not comfortable turning this project over to someone with limited experience even though we liked and saw great potential in him. After further consideration, the committee agreed. However, we did commit internally to hire him for future MFE projects that were more suitable for him.

The lesson was that while it is important to make an honest, strategic effort to identify and hire a diverse workforce or staff, it cannot be the only determining factor. If all things are equal, or maybe even not quite equal as far as experience and background, if you are committed to diversity in your organization, you should hire the person who adds diversity. Diversifying your organization sometimes requires you to stretch and make accommodations to give a chance to people who heretofore may not have had such an opportunity. But that only applies to a certain degree. If the difference between the two candidates is as stark as it was in this case, you must make the decision that best serves your organization and its constituency. I also believe it was the best decision for him as it wouldn't have done anyone any good if he failed on the project. No one wins in that situation.

That said, we would not have confronted and learned from this situation unless, as an organization, we hadn't been committed to becoming more diverse. We also learned that making the commitment doesn't assure immediate, tangible results. If you are committed to the concept as a long-term goal, it might take time to build the contacts and connections that will eventually result in concrete progress. In this case, while we did not hire the young man for this project, we were impressed with him and put him on our radar screen for future projects. Our network of potential vendors of color had widened.

To that end, shortly thereafter, I met him for drinks to learn more about him and to begin to develop a relationship. I wanted to keep the door open. And, good thing, as we eventually hired him for a different project. And he knocked the assignment out of the ballpark! We loved his work. And for an even better ending, we ended up hiring him as the graphic designer for volume four in the Songs For Justice series. Again, he did a great job and we have continued to hire him for additional projects. I've even hired him for a personal, non-MFE project. In fact, we've come to think so highly of him that we recruited him to serve on our board. Sometimes it takes time for all the stars to align.

As a result of our targeted efforts, our POC network has continued to expand. That's progress we feel pretty good about. But it wouldn't have happened without our original commitment to become a more diverse organization and our willingness to build on that commitment brick by brick over the course of time, even if it meant having to navigate sensitive and fraught issues along the way.

## ANOTHER POTHOLE ON THE ROAD TO PROGRESS

Another jarring wake-up call occurred as we were choosing the civil and human rights speeches for the side B of each record. As mentioned, each record highlights specific groups and the issues they face regarding justice and equity. This lesson occurred on the record slated to feature women's right to vote. My research turned up a speech by Susan B. Anthony. It was perfect, or so I thought. We recorded the speech and, while the record was on its way to being pressed, the CBO we were featuring on that record told us they were not willing to be associated with Susan B. Anthony. Why? Because while she advocated for women's right to vote, the right of Black women to vote was an afterthought, at best. In fact, White led suffragist organizations sometimes made Black women march at the back of suffrage parades.

I had no idea. Neither did other members of the selection committee, including members of color.

Why didn't we know this? What subjects and issues do our schools cover and address in American history? This is a significant part of our nation's history left unexplored. We'll take a closer look at the history taught in our schools and who exactly writes that history later.

Fortunately, we were educated on this important fact before embarrassing ourselves publicly. We regrouped and began to identify alternative speeches. Clearly, we had to be more thorough, strategic, and directed in the materials we'd feature. But again, a lesson was learned and not only is the project better because of it, so is the organization. Rather than talking about it or simply writing a social justice statement, we were doing something knowing we'd make mistakes along the way. As T. S. Eliott said, "Only those who will risk going too far can possibly find out how far one can go." The Susan B. Anthony experience clued us to how challenging it would be to select historical figures and speeches to feature.

## CANCELLING BOOKER T. WASHINGTON

Booker T. Washington (1856-1915) was one of the most important and influential educators in our nation's history. It is no stretch to say that no one has been more directly responsible for providing access to educational opportunity for Black Americans. For that reason, I proposed we feature a speech of his titled, "Democracy and Education." No one on the committee objected. We proceeded to have it read and recorded.

In a subsequent meeting, while discussing speeches to feature, a member raised an objection.

Washington believed the quickest way to improve the quality of Black life was to work with Whites, temporarily accepting elements of segregation and discrimination as the best way to achieve long-term economic benefits. He advocated vocational education as a pragmatic way for Blacks to improve their lives over time. In some circles, his focus on educating Blacks in the trades as one avenue for them to gain employment, build wealth, and ultimately power was seen as appeasement and accommodation to the existing racist status quo.

W.E.B. DuBois (1868-1963), the towering Black intellectual, scholar, and political activist had a different notion about achieving equality. DuBois embraced assimilation and saw higher education as the vehicle to achieve it. He believed that it would be the top Black intellectuals who would lead Black Americans to a better life. He referred to them as the "Talented Tenth." He thought that achieving access to higher education would result in the development of the Talented Tenth, who would then provide leadership to the rest of the Black community, resulting in the achievement of equality.

I am no historian, and this is a broad-brush treatment of the debate between these two influential educational leaders regarding how best to achieve social and economic equality. Regardless, when the question of Washington's perceived "appeasement" was raised, the mood and direction of the committee discussion changed dramatically. Within fifteen minutes, the debate went from using the speech to cancelling it. The concern was that featuring Washington would create controversy that could alienate people. I couldn't believe what had transpired. The fact was that none of us were what you would consider scholars or experts on this aspect of Black history. Yet, in the space of fifteen minutes we had "cancelled" Booker T. Washington. This was disturbing because I felt it deserved more thoughtful discussion and consideration. I asked to schedule another call to make certain it was the path we wanted to pursue. Agonizing over what to do, I researched more deeply the theories and history of these great men. I sent background information to the committee and encouraged them to review it before we reconvened.

After finishing the research, I delivered a memo to the committee setting forth my take on the issue. It seemed to me there could be several approaches, each effective in its own way, to leverage the educational system to lift Black Americans to a better place. Further, Washington was not opposed to higher education as a tool for Black advancement as he quietly provided funding to support DuBois's efforts around the issue of access to higher education for Black Americans. He also founded what is now Tuskegee University. It seemed logical to me that there was room for both approaches, each unique but each seeking the same goal.

Another concern was whether not getting it exactly right was worth not doing it at all because we were afraid it might ruffle a few feathers. If we only featured safe speeches and historical figures who we and others were comfortable with, there would be no dialogue, no increased understanding and, as a result, nothing would change.

I also believed that the subjects and concerns Washington addressed in the speech were more important than ever as his focus was on educating Blacks in the trades as one avenue to gain employment and build wealth and power. Further, given the debate at the time around President Joe Biden's education plan, those concerns were timely. Specifically, Biden's plan called for providing two years of community college and/or trade school for free. At the core of this policy is providing opportunities to learn a skill or trade that can lead to a solid middle-class life. We were having the same debate today that Washington and DuBois were having back in the 1890s. Yes, higher education is one avenue to lift people up. But so too are the trades. There is no shame in building a career in the trades.

Further, it was a speech about the interrelation among education, voting rights, and democracy. Washington wrote about the importance of education as the means to develop an informed citizenry, which contributes to a more just and vibrant democracy. Given all that is going on in our country regarding voter rights and voter suppression, his speech resonates today. For those reasons, I believed this man, his ideas, and that speech could provide a powerful platform and construct to allow us to do exactly what the Songs For Justice project was all about—generating debate around difficult issues in the hope of educating and ultimately inspiring others to action.

In the end, my arguments did not carry the day as the committee decided to identify another speech and person to feature. It was a challenging moment with no clear answer, just another significant bump in the road. That said, challenges also present opportunities to grow and learn. Here are the lessons I learned from this experience, some relating to race and others to leadership.

First, never take for granted the direction a discussion might take. When people convene to make decisions, events can take unexpected twists and turns, leaving you in a place that you had not expected. When that occurs, regroup, reassess, and figure out where to go from there.

Second, be mindful about how fraught, challenging, and explosive discussions around race can be. Given our nation's history, that is no surprise. Regardless, it was one of those moments where I said to myself, *"What have we gotten ourselves into?"* I questioned whether it was worth all the personal angst I was experiencing and risk we, as an organization, were assuming. But then you realize that the angst and risk is nothing compared to the 24/7/365/400+ challenges that Blacks have faced. While it was a bump in the road, it was one that we had to overcome, move forward and, in the words of Martin Luther King, Jr., "keep our eyes on the prize."

Third, an executive director or someone in a comparable leadership position must find balance in making organizational decisions. In the case of BTW speech, I disagreed with the final decision but did not fight it. As a leader, pick your battles and embrace decisions that don't always go your way for the betterment of the organization.

## A CLUELESS OLD WHITE DUDE

Another misstep and hard lesson learned occurred when attempting to recruit a spoken word artist to contribute to the project. For the issues featured in each record, we attempted to match people with the corresponding ethnicity or sexual orientation. For example, the people we featured in the record highlighting LGBTQ+ rights and issues were all people who identify as members of the LGBTQ+ community.

In seeking potential contributors for a record to feature issues affecting the Hispanic/Latino community, several people mentioned a woman of Hispanic descent as an excellent potential contributor. I set about trying to recruit her specifically for that record. During our discussion, she mentioned that while her father was Hispanic, she identified more as a Black Queer woman because her mother was Black. I didn't "hear," let alone fully understand, what she was getting at. I suggested something to the effect of, "Maybe this might be an opportunity to do some thinking and research and create some new spoken word material around your Hispanic heritage." I was thinking of it as an opportunity to expand her repertoire. My response was completely tone deaf and hurtful. This was not about me or my agenda. We continued our conversation during which she mentioned it again. Eventually, a lightbulb went off in my head, "Ah, okay, I get it." I said, "That's okay. We'll have you contribute to a future record where we highlight issues you identify with most." After hanging up, I thought we had reached an understanding.

Not so fast.

Little did I know how disrespectful I had been. I was, without realizing it and with no ill intent, insensitive and in the wrong. The next morning, I woke up to find that she had posted on social media her displeasure that an "Old White Dude" had suggested she "research" her Hispanic heritage. To her credit, she didn't leave the post up long. But she had made her point in a very public way. She withdrew from the project. I was horrified. While my intent was pure, my specific action was misguided. I emailed her and apologized profusely. That said, being called out publicly for being an "Old White Dude" provided the inspiration for this book. It's another example of how a defeat, challenge, or a "calling out" can present unexpected opportunities.

This incident offered another lesson we OWDs should consider. My reaction to her attempted explanation of her preference was to apply my personal experiences or mindset (a chance to develop additional "material") to her reality. It was an instance of my White privilege shining through. We need to realize that whatever the situation, we all bring and apply our own experiences and backgrounds to the situations we face. This is to be expected. However, we must also make room for and consider the collective experiences and backgrounds of POC in those situations.

Perhaps the most potent example of this is when police pull over drivers for DWB, "driving while Black." While I can attest that being pulled over by the police is not a comfortable experience, for a Black person, it must be terrifying. Two totally different perspectives, both shaped by the personal and historical experiences at the hands of police officers. In other words, we should not let our personal experiences as White men of privilege cloud our understanding of, or empathy toward, the experiences of POC. Rather, we should respect and take those experiences into account as they are all too real for Black Americans.

Throughout this project I have been *schooled* on many other issues and behaviors, mostly around the use of language. Phrases that, in the past, might have been used in an off-handed way, have now become points of contention we must pay attention to. The use and importance of language around racial issues has become much more nuanced. While this represents progress, it can be challenging. For example, during a meeting of our steering committee, I was called out for using the term "handicapped people." I was gently informed that the term is no longer used and that the appropriate term was "people with disabilities." I thanked the person who called me out, made a mental note of it, and committed myself to never make that mistake again. A small thing, perhaps, but it's progress.

Here are two more examples. Before engaging in this project, I had limited appreciation for the diversity that exists in the Hispanic/Latino communities. The Hispanic/Latino diaspora is varied, consisting of Puerto Ricans, Mexicans, Cubans, Dominicans, Colombians, and Panamanians, among others, each with their own histories, customs, and cultures. My guess is that most North Americans are not aware of this. In my case, I had not given it any thought.

And something else we have done as an organization that never would have occurred to us without the 360-degree evaluation of our operations and programs involved our website. We decided to upgrade our website to where it can be accessed and read in both English and Spanish. That is something we should have figured out long ago. While most of the children we serve speak English, often their parents or guardians do not. That simple adjustment, a result of our directed efforts to become more inclusive and diverse, made us more family friendly for Spanish speaking families and thus a much more effective organization.

And here's a side note about cluelessness around these issues. While clueless is certainly an apt descriptor, I came across another term that we can use to describe ourselves. In his excellent book, *How the Word is Passed: A Reckoning with the History of Slavery Across America,* Clint Smith quoted a term used by John Cummings. Cummings bought and restored the Whitney Plantation in Wallace, Louisiana, into a museum/ exhibit which he uses to tell the story of the slave plantation as well as the 1811 slave rebellion led by Charles Deslondes. When he comes across some hidden history regarding these issues and asks, as I have throughout this book, "Why didn't I know that? I should have known that." Rather than that being considered "clueless," he offers a kinder, gentler term, "discovered ignorance." (Smith 2021, 77)

Regardless, my education, or discovered ignorance, continues.

## CEDING POWER

"Come on, John. Pass the ball."

As the Davidson College career leader in shots taken, I've heard that before. It's not surprising as I never met a shot I didn't like. But it was a bit surprising to hear that plea during a Zoom call with a committee that was strategizing regarding what types of events and activities we might want to conduct in conjunction with the release of various SFJ records.

The committee was very diverse, including young POC. As mentioned, one of the major benefits of MFE taking on the SFJ project, and our commitment to diversify, was it introduced us to a wide variety of talented musicians, artists, designers, poets, and spoken word artists, mostly POC. While we still have a long way to go, we have made significant progress throughout our entire internal structure.

We've taken two important steps in this regard. The first, to make that conscious organizational decision and second, to begin to actively recruit and place POC in these positions. While we are proud of that decision and our follow-up, I have since come to realize that those were only the first two steps necessary to achieve meaningful progress and change. There is another critical step that must follow. While it is great to have POC on your board or in your organization, that is not enough unless you begin to actively involve those POC in various decision-making and operational processes in meaningful ways. In other words, as White leaders of an organization, we must be willing to cede power.

"Nothing about us without us" is a phrase coined by James Charlton, who authored a book by the same name. Charlton was referencing the struggles of people with disabilities to be heard and have their concerns and challenges acknowledged and addressed. His statement advances the conviction that people with disabilities know what is best for themselves. The same principle applies to POC and issues around race. While Whites can certainly be allies and advocates for social justice, it is not enough. The next critical step is to reach out and facilitate a partnership with POC in sharing the road to inclusion and equity.

But that is easier said than done. To do so, we must be willing to cede a measure of power. It's not easy to convince people to cede power, particularly with such a long history of White men in particular working to maintain the status quo power structure. As Martin Luther King wrote in his "Letter from Birmingham Jail," "History is the long and tragic story that privileged groups seldom give up their privilege voluntarily. Individuals may see the moral light and voluntarily give up their unjust posture, but as Reinhold Niebuhr has reminded us, groups are more immoral than individuals."

Not only must Whites be willing to cede power, we must also be willing to work under POC leadership. Whether as an individual or an organization, to achieve real progress on social justice and equity, we must be willing to move along the spectrum of allyship to partnership.

When it was suggested during the Zoom call by that young POC that I pass the ball, he was referring to me letting him serve as the lead person on the committee to organize and conduct a series of events. Admittedly, I was a bit hesitant. He was young and I did not have a lot of experience with him as an organizer and leader. There was also a bit of "founder's syndrome" lurking in the back of my mind as MFE has been my baby and, for the most part, I have had a strong hand in virtually everything the organization has done. But what was the point of committing to diversity and recruiting POC to be a part of the MFE team if I was unwilling to give them the opportunity to contribute in a concrete, meaningful way? I had to let go and cede some power and authority to make that commitment to diversity become a reality. In short, committing to diversity is a first step and a relatively easy one compared to the challenge of sharing, in meaningful ways, power and authority.

So, I passed him the ball. Another lesson learned.

The opportunity to create and work on our Songs For Justice project has been one of the most challenging, but also rewarding, journeys I have ever embarked upon. My learning curve around issues of race and equity has been enormous. I've also learned much about communication, collaboration, discipline, persistence, personal responsibility, creativity, and leadership. These are all skills and characteristics required to be a successful teammate, bandmate, fellow worker as well as a positive force for social justice.

And the lessons learned will continue to inform and influence that ongoing journey, as you will see in the pages to follow.

CHAPTER SIX

# DOING THE WORK: THE TRUTH SHALL SET YOU FREE

*"The truth will set you free, but first it will piss you off."*
—Gloria Steinem

It's time to do the work. And that work starts with White folks no longer complaining about how we feel so burdened by having to, for the first time in our lives, pay attention to issues of race in a more thoughtful, nuanced, and concerted way. It's time for us to stop whining about how we must think about the things we say and do around the issue of race. Or how we are worried about saying or doing something offensive and being called out for it. Or how, when in the past we simply proceeded with a hiring decision, we now must provide equal consideration of a POC.

And let's not throw out those tired memes about having to "go slow," "take our time," or "be patient." Be patient? Go slow? For whom? Isn't over 400 years long enough? Asking for patience is deflecting from the issue and protects our White privilege. In the words of Martin Luther King, Jr., from his "Letter from Birmingham Jail", "I have heard the word 'wait.' It rings in the ear of every Negro with a piercing familiarity. This 'wait' has always meant 'never'." Or, the legal maxim, 'Justice delayed is justice denied.'"

Yes, we know we did not participate in the brutal legacy of slavery and the practices of the Jim Crow era. But as White people we have reaped the privilege of that dark legacy. That legacy is about keeping in place a system designed to maintain White, male privilege in everything from health care to housing to education to criminal justice.

Still don't believe it? I've heard the narratives and arguments asserting that civil rights laws have changed everything and how everyone now has equal opportunity. Yes, those civil rights laws have made a difference. But to think they have erased the harm, scars, hate, and inequalities of the past? Hardly! Plus, that's too easy. That narrative allows us to avoid any responsibility to work on making those rights and opportunities a reality. It allows us to wash our hands of the entire issue. It provides all the justification we need to complain about others "getting things" that for 400 years, like the bathrooms, water fountains, and lunch counters during slavery and Jim Crow, had been for Whites only.

The reality of America in 2023 is that White privilege has not gone anywhere. In virtually every segment of our lives and society, discrimination remains rampant. Yes, systemic racism still exists in the United States.

Still not convinced. Well, the following four chapters, as well as the narrated bibliography at the end of the book, are for you because it's clear that we've all got some work to do. It is designed to get you started. Why is this important? Because those who hold the levers of power, Old White Dudes, have written that history. It is a history that has been whitewashed and downplayed the challenges facing Blacks in a racist society as well as the role that Blacks have played in building our nation.

Let's be clear. The history taught in America falls woefully short of an honest, unvarnished account of racism in America, particularly the dark institutions of slavery, Jim Crow, as well as the civil rights era. Not only does our historical account of Black history gloss over or ignore the dark side of the Black experience, but it also barely acknowledges that the American economy, especially in the pre-Civil War South, had been generated largely off the backs of free Black labor. The teaching of American history barely acknowledges how Blacks have played a major contributing role in virtually every aspect of American life, from childcare to manual labor to entertainment to culture to service in the military. We have been raised and taught that, other than athletes and entertainers, Blacks have contributed little of value to the growth and prosperity of our country. The fact is that if you write the history, you tend to write a version that sheds the most positive light upon yourself. It's human nature.

Or, in the words of Martin Luther King's, *Where Do We Go from Here: Chaos or Community?* "The tendency to ignore the Negro's contribution to American life and to strip him of his personhood is as old as the earliest history books and as contemporary as the morning's newspaper." (King 1968, 44)

Why is it so important that we highlight and examine the history of the Black experience in America? What is the purpose of doing the work to dig out the truth from under the historical rocks that have been written forever by the White male establishment? *Lies My Teacher Told Me: Everything Your American History Textbook Got Wrong*, written by James W. Loewen, provides some important context. He points out that unless we acknowledge and understand our history, there is little chance that we will be able to ever right the wrongs of that history. Without a truthful, honest, unvarnished understanding of the past, we'll never be able to recognize and address the challenges of the present and future.

He writes, "First, the truth can set us free. That is, when we understand what really happened in the past, then we know what to do to cause our nation to remedy its problems in the present. The truth is, for example, that African Americans and Native Americans are not less intelligent than European Americans and Asian Americans. They test that way, true, but underlying the disappointing test results are social causes, including test bias and educational and social inequities, that we can readily fix. So, we do not need to fear the truth.

"Second, there is a reciprocal relationship between truth about the past and justice in the present. When we achieve justice in the present, remedying some past event or practice, then we can face it and talk about it more openly, precisely because we have made it right. It has become a success story . . .

" . . . Conversely, a topic that is mystified or distorted in our history, like secession, usually signifies a continuing injustice in the present, like racism. Telling the truth about the past can help us make it right from here on." (Loewen 1995, 2007, 2018, xix and xx.)

Loewen quotes Maya Angelou, who wrote,

"History, despite its wrenching pain,

Cannot be unlived, and if faced

With courage, need not be lived again." (Loewen 1995, 2007, 2018, 134)

Hopefully, the resources identified and briefly summarized will help you begin your social justice work. To that end, in the four chapters to follow, I identify four influential thinkers/writers and their works that have had a profound impact on my education and thinking on these issues. These works were highlighted because I found them to not only be compelling but also, taken together, they provide a general view of some of the fundamental issues and challenges we are facing in the fight for racial justice and equity. But there are so many more resources that can further inform your thinking and knowledge base. That being the case, I encourage you to also read the narrated bibliography where several additional resources are offered for consideration.

Now that you have started your personal journey to better understand these issues by reading this book, my hope is that reading these summaries and observations will pique your interest to learn more and continue down the road on your own journey of self-discovery and hopefully, change. And when you do continue down that road, what might you find?

In my own efforts of self-discovery around issues of race, I found that I was not as blameless and progressive as I had thought. But to some degree, that is understandable when we live in a segregated world fully protected by our White privilege. There's no shame in admitting that. The question is whether you choose to do something about it.

Folks who are infinitely more knowledgeable may take issue with some of my impressions, thoughts, and conclusions. This is inevitable as the Black experience in this country is as vast, complex, and nuanced as US history itself. The two are forever and completely intertwined.

While there is room to respectfully disagree on some issues, there is a lot more that we should be able to agree upon. History and facts, no matter how sordid or unnerving, don't lie. Included are perspectives of scholars who study these issues and that history, placing events into a broader perspective to challenge us to do better. There are also eyewitness accounts and stories passed down and documented through the years, stories that are so vivid and compelling as to leave you feeling a wide array of emotions—disbelief, anger, revulsion, and shame. Other times you will be amazed, inspired, and hopeful. There are stories and narratives we must not simply listen to but thoughtfully consider. Our histories are intertwined. Hearing the stories and learning that unvarnished truth is the first step in breaking the chains of injustice, intolerance, and hate.

As the title of this chapter suggests, it's time for us White folks to begin to "do the work." Clearly, you have already made the decision to begin to do the work as you decided to read this book. In doing so, you are, hopefully, considering taking the next step of taking action to become a force for justice.

# CHAPTER SEVEN

# EDDIE GLAUDE, JR.

*"Not everything that is faced can be changed, but nothing can be changed until it is faced."*

—James Baldwin

L et's begin our work with *Begin Again: James Baldwin's America and the Urgent Lessons for Our Own*, written by Princeton University professor Eddie Glaude, Jr. This is a fascinating look at the writings and life of James Baldwin. Baldwin (1924-1987) was one of the twentieth century's greatest writers and playwrights. He was especially known for his exploration of racial and social issues and for his essays on the Black experience in America.

This was one of the first books I read after George Floyd's murder. It's a helpful starting place because Glaude creates a broad historical framework regarding the ebbs and flows of the history of race and civil rights in America. According to Glaude, there have been three times in the history of our nation where it seemed as if there was real opportunity to live up to the promise of justice for all. The first was at the conclusion of the Civil War (1865) when Confederate secession ended and slavery was abolished, making the newly freed slaves citizens with civil rights ostensibly guaranteed, and marking the beginning of the era known as Reconstruction. Unfortunately, this new world for Black Americans didn't last very long. The moment Blacks began to take advantage of their newfound civil rights, a backlash brewed against such progress, particularly in the South. The Reconstruction period effectively ended in practice in 1877 with the election of Republican

Rutherford B. Hayes as president after striking a deal with Southern Democrats to withdraw all remaining federal troops from the South. With federal troops no longer in place to ensure those rights, Whites were able to go back to doing what they did before Reconstruction, except for outright slavery.

The final nail in the coffin of Reconstruction was the 1896 Supreme Court decision in *Plessy vs. Ferguson*, which held that state-mandated segregation did not violate the US Constitution, giving rise to the "separate but equal" doctrine in American jurisprudence and permitting states to adopt laws of their choosing as applied to civil rights. That spawned a series of state sponsored Jim Crow laws that mandated racial segregation in all public facilities, primarily in the states of the former Confederacy. As a result, theaters, restaurants, transportation, and schools, once again, became legally segregated. *Plessy* remained the controlling law until 1954 when the Supreme Court in *Brown vs Board of Education of Topeka*, overturned it, thus starting the process of ending legalized segregation.

Next, Glaude moves on to the civil rights era (mid-1960s), which he describes as the second promising watershed moment in our nation's civil rights journey. Most significant was the passage of the Civil Rights Act of 1964, which prohibited discrimination based on race, color, religion, sex, or national origin. That federal legislation prohibited discrimination in public accommodations and federally funded programs and strengthened the enforcement of voting rights and the desegregation of schools. But in a replay of the Reconstruction era, White backlash reared its ugly head driven by fear of the erosion of privilege that Whites had come to view as their right alone. The White power structure fought back. This time, the main weapon used was the so-called *war on drugs*.

In June 1971, President Richard Nixon declared a "war on drugs." He dramatically increased the size and presence of federal drug control agencies, pushing through measures such as mandatory sentencing and no-knock warrants. But at its core, this wasn't a war on drugs. It was a different way to establish control over Black Americans. Consider this quote from John Ehrlichman, a top Nixon aide at the time.

"You want to know what this was really all about? The Nixon campaign in 1968, and the Nixon White House after that, had two enemies: the antiwar left and black people. You understand what I'm saying? We knew we couldn't make it illegal to be either against the war or blacks, but by getting the public to associate the hippies with marijuana and blacks with heroin, and then criminalizing both heavily, we could disrupt those communities. We could arrest their leaders, raid their homes, break up their meetings, and vilify them night after night on the evening news. Did we know we were lying about the drugs? Of course, we did." https://drugpolicy.org/issues/brief-history-drug-war

In short, this was Jim Crow in disguise.

And it didn't stop with Nixon. In 1982, Ronald Reagan doubled down on the war on drugs. The cynical and destructive nature of that war is extremely disturbing. But given our history as a nation regarding racism, it's not surprising. To bring the implications and impact of this "war" into sharper focus, we turn to Michelle Alexander, author of *The New Jim Crow: Mass Incarceration in the Age of Colorblindness,* perhaps the most definitive book on the subject and deserves to be quoted at length.

"Most people assume the War on Drugs was launched in response to the crisis caused by crack cocaine in inner-city neighborhoods. This view holds that the racial disparities in drug convictions and sentences, as well as the rapid explosion of the prison population, reflects nothing more than the government's zealous—but benign—efforts to address rampant drug crime in poor, minority neighborhoods. This view, while understandable, given the sensational media coverage of crack in the 1980s and 1990s, is simply wrong. While it is true that the publicity surrounding crack cocaine led to a dramatic increase in funding for the drug war (as well as sentencing policies that greatly exacerbated racial disparities in incarceration rates), there is no truth to the notion that the War on Drugs was launched in response to crack cocaine. President

Reagan announced the current drug war in 1982, before crack cocaine became an issue in the media or a crisis in poor black neighborhoods. A few years after the drug war was declared, crack began to spread rapidly in the poor black neighborhoods of Los Angeles and later emerged in cities across the country. The Reagan administration hired staff to publicize the emergence of crack cocaine in 1985 as part of a strategic effort to build public and legislative support for the war. The media campaign was an extraordinary success. Almost overnight, the media was saturated with images of Black "crack whores," "crack dealers" and "crack babies"— images that seemed to confirm the worst negative racial stereotypes about impoverished inner-city residents. The media bonanza surrounding the new 'demon drug' helped catapult the War on Drugs from an ambitious federal policy to an actual war." (Alexander 2020, 6)

The desire to "control" the Black population did not end and in far too many ways continues today. The only change is the chosen methodology. The forms of oppression have simply evolved.

And if two major White backlash events to roll back progress regarding justice for Black Americans were not enough, according to Glaude, we are currently enmeshed in a third. This time in response to the election of Barack Obama. After Obama was elected, White nationalism and voter suppression efforts began to rise. This time Jim Crow returned disguised as Donald Trump who stoked fear of the *other* and rode that backlash into the White House. It has only increased since.

That said, a case can also be made that we are currently in a period of positive change regarding attitudes about race, as an increasing number of Americans are coming to grips with the nation's deep and systemic racism. It was notable, for example, that of those who marched to protest of George Floyd's death (and far too many similar Black victims), many Whites marched as well.

Nonetheless, it is hard to ignore the emergence, or perhaps better said, re-emergence, of a White nationalist movement founded on perceptions of racial superiority and fueled with fear of POC. Once the province of fringe groups, White nationalists have increasingly infiltrated the mainstream political narrative, the media, and institutions. Our political dialogue has evolved from the Jim Crow bullhorn to coded "dog whistle" language to spew their hate. Trump provided cover and legitimacy to this language and related beliefs and, as a result, the White nationalist movement in our country is growing.

According to the FBI, the greatest terrorist threat in the US is no longer from foreign actors, but rather domestic terrorist groups, most of which espouse White nationalism. We all witnessed that terrifying reality during the January 6, 2021, insurrection to overturn the results of an election and the peaceful transfer of power at the nation's capital.

The fundamental lesson from Glaude's work that stuck with me is that there is a substantial proportion of Whites who simply cannot accept POC gaining rights and will fight to dismantle any such progress. They believe that America is "theirs" and thus should be a White-centric society. It is a pattern that has repeated itself throughout our nation's history. As a result of organized and targeted backlash, progress retrenches. Two steps forward and one step back.

Charles M. Blow mentioned this in several *New York Times* columns. For example, in "After the Trial, One Battle is Won. The War Continues" (April 23, 2021, A-25), he made this comment about the guilty verdict against Derek Chauvin for the murder of George Floyd. "History has been a stern instructor of Black people in this country, beating out hope whenever it dares emerge. As James Baldwin once put it, imbedded in the American Negro is the 'wise desire not to be betrayed by too much hoping.' The possessor of dashed hopes is in some ways more injured and dangerous than the consistently hopeless. The possessors of dashed hopes spread their wings, which makes them vulnerable, and gets them clipped. Bitterness is a natural byproduct of such betrayal." And then this in "Learning Caution from a Late Columnist" (April 26, 2021, A-20). "No matter how hopeful the moment, no matter how great the advance, never— ever— underestimate white supremacy."

That was a simplified recap of Glaude's work, which deserves a more thorough treatment than what is offered here. Regardless, *Begin Again* is a great place to begin the process of learning more about the history of the Black experience in America.

# CHAPTER EIGHT

# ROBIN DIANGELO

*"The only thing we have to fear is fear itself."*
—Franklin D. Roosevelt

From Glaude we will move to two books by a White writer, Robin DiAngelo. *White Fragility: Why it's so Hard for White People to Talk About Racism* and her follow-up, titled, *Nice Racism: How Progressive White People Perpetuate Racial Harm*. DiAngelo used the term "White fragility" to describe defensiveness that White people exhibit when their ideas about racism and equity are challenged and, when they feel implicated in White supremacy. This is perhaps the most significant factor in holding back progress around issues of race and justice. While some may think racism is a "Black problem," the fact is, we White folks are the problem. Our inability to embrace that reality is what stymies progress. Simply put, Blacks have endured over 400 years of brutal discrimination but whenever our complicity in creating and maintaining that system is challenged, we freak out. We collapse. We withdraw. We do anything but face the truth.

In the words of Martin Luther King, "Negroes only hold one key to the double lock of peaceful change. The other is in the hands of the white community." (Quote referenced by Vincent Harding in his Introduction to *Where Do We Go from Here? Chaos or Community?* King 1968, xxii)

DiAngelo offers up the story of Jackie Robinson for consideration.

"The story of Jackie Robinson is a classic example of how whiteness obscures racism by rendering whites, white privilege, and racist institutions invisible. Robinson is often celebrated as the first African

American to break the color line and play in major league baseball. While Robinson was certainly an amazing baseball player, this story line depicts him as racially special, a black man who broke the color line himself. The subtext is that Robinson finally had what it took to play with whites, as if no black athlete before him was strong enough to compete at that level. Imagine if instead, the story went something like this: 'Jackie Robinson, the first black man whites allowed to play major-league baseball.' This version makes a critical distinction because no matter how fantastic a baseball player Robinson was, he simply could not play in the major leagues if whites—who controlled the institution—did not allow it. Were he to walk onto the field before being granted permission by white owners and policy makers, the police would have removed him." (DiAngelo 2018, 26)

In other words, White men have established, maintained, and held the keys to the doors of our nation's institutions, whether educational, athletic, economic, or political, to name only a few. As such, it is ultimately up to us White dudes to reform those institutions and disrupt the status quo.

Another nice feature of her work is that both of her books provide study guides with questions to consider, as well as additional resources to read and access.

While DiAngelo offers a harsh, but needed dose of reality, she also provides space for growth. I liked her thoughts on how we are all on our own racial continuum, and that becoming more sensitive to and aware of our racism is a process and journey. This is not something we can switch on and off. It takes time and effort. But there is a path forward. We must acknowledge our White privilege and then commit to doing the necessary work to educate ourselves to move further along on our personal continuum and journey.

# CHAPTER NINE

## HEATHER MCGHEE

*"Sometimes when you sacrifice something precious, you're not really losing it. You're just passing it on to someone else."*

—Mitch Albom

Another book that was foundational in my research and understanding of these issues was *The Sum of Us: What Racism Costs Everyone and How We Can Prosper Together*, by Heather McGhee. This book was a real eye opener. McGhee's area of expertise is the economy. She explores the centuries-long resistance of White people, particularly White men, to anything that results in economic support, benefits, resources, or opportunities for Black Americans. She takes a sweeping look at various economic factors from rising student debt to the 2008 financial crisis, among others. She writes that the common theme throughout is racism. She also makes a compelling case that many of the policies and practices that deny economic opportunity to Blacks also negatively impact Whites.

McGhee explains that barriers to progress regarding justice and equity are the result of the distorted mindset of many Whites around providing government benefits or legal assistance to POC. Examples include affirmative action measures, access to public resources, and social services and benefits. She notes that often it is not simply that Whites object to benefits or opportunities that, in their minds, are "handouts" to undeserving Blacks. McGhee writes that when it comes to race, we are engaged in a zero-sum game. Specifically, if people of color are provided benefits or opportunities, those are benefits or opportunities that are being taken away from Whites. The notion of a rising tide raising all ships, or that if my neighbor is doing better, ultimately, so am I, holds no currency with far too many Whites.

McGhee uses swimming pools as an example. In the 1950s and 1960s, hundreds of towns and municipalities built public swimming pools. They were a source of community pride and brought people and families together for fun, exercise, and fellowship. Of course, being the 1950s and 60s, most public swimming pools were for Whites only. But then came the Civil Rights Act of the mid 1960s, which eliminated racial discrimination in public facilities. Blacks were now allowed to swim in the pools. But rather than doing the difficult work as a community to integrate the pools, many communities closed them, and, in some reported cases, filled them with concrete. Rather than allowing access to Black members of their community, Whites decided that no one would be able to swim in what were wonderful community assets. They were denying Blacks access to that community resource and in the process eliminating their own access, often in far greater numbers.

Talk about cutting off your nose to spite your face!

That attitude continues to this day. A good example is the provision in President Obama's Affordable Care Act (ACA) that allowed states to expand eligibility to receive Medicaid benefits. Beginning in 2014, the ACA offered states the option to expand eligibility for Medicaid to individuals with incomes up to 138 percent of the federal poverty level, with the federal government providing all the cost of newly eligible enrollees. That percentage dropped to 90 percent in 2020 where it will remain. At most, states will be responsible for 10 percent of the added cost. Why would states, (all of which have Republican governors and Republican controlled state legislatures) deny this opportunity to reduce the number of uninsured? You can't help but wonder if one of the drivers of such policies is the notion of the "zero-sum paradigm." Again, it's not simply poor Black folks who would benefit from this expansion, but many poor White folks would as well. Again, likely in greater numbers.

Why would public officials turn down an opportunity to provide more health care coverage and services at virtually no cost? Think about that! Denying fellow Americans, Black and, even more in raw numbers, Whites,' access to affordable health care. How does ensuring that a sizable segment of our fellow American families will be less healthy lift you up? What kind of cruel, heartless society have we become?

The false narrative the White male power structure has concocted, promoted, and maintained is that Blacks are lazy and don't deserve a hand up through public assistance. It is such a powerful narrative that many poor White people, who could benefit from the expanded Medicaid coverage, buy into it.

In short, one of the methods the White male establishment employs to retain wealth, power, and privilege is pitting Blacks and poor and middle-class Whites against each other. If you keep the masses bickering among themselves, they will be too busy arguing and vilifying each other to notice, let along organize against, income inequality and social injustice.

This is explored in Tim Wise's work *White Like Me: Reflections on Race from a Privileged Son*, a memoir in which he explores how racist privilege shapes the lives of White Americans in employment, education housing, criminal justice, among other areas and in that way pits "poor Whites and Blacks against each other." He refers to it as the "psychological wage of whiteness," which Black scholar W.E.B. DuBois coined, and which "allowed struggling white folks to accept their miserable lot in life, so long as they were doing better than Blacks. To the White masses in [KKK leader David] Duke country, they had more in common with the multi-millionaires along St. Charles Avenue and on Audubon Place (the wealthiest street in the city) than with African Americans, struggling for opportunities much as they were. Racial bonding took priority over class unity, or in this case, common sense. . . . So, for the past several years, struggling white folks had cast their lot with racism—all so as to make themselves feel superior to somebody, *anybody* . . ." (Wise 2008, 2011, 166 -7)

Again, my treatment of McGhee's work is very broad. But her core concept of how the existing White, male establishment has created and sold the lie of economic and social policy as a zero-sum game was enlightening. It certainly added to my understanding of the various impacts of economic policy on racism.

Something I have never understood is how anyone can be so selfish to think that if their neighbor is doing better somehow that means they are worse off. It does not have to be *us versus them*. The fact is, if my neighbor is doing better, so am I.

# CHAPTER TEN

## MICHELE ALEXANDER

*"To deny people their human rights is to challenge their very humanity."*

—Nelson Mandela

And then there is the previously mentioned Michelle Alexander's *The New Jim Crow: Mass Incarceration in the Age of Colorblindness.* This book exposed my ignorance of the unjust workings of our criminal justice system. She does an excellent job of laying out the extent and impacts of that cruel system. Of note is a quote she used from human rights champion Bryan Stevenson, who observed that "slavery didn't end; it evolved."

Alexander goes on to discuss how mass incarceration became a different form of slavery. "The politics of White supremacy, which defined our original constitution, have continued unabated— repeatedly and predictably engendering new systems of racial and social control . . . The very same playbook has been used over and over in this country by those who seek to preserve racial hierarchy, or to exploit racial resentments and anxiety for political gain, each time with similar results." (Alexander 2020, xiv, xv)

The mass incarceration system in America is corrupt to the core. But here's the key. She writes, "it is the 'prison label, not the prison time' that matters most if we are to understand the true scope of mass incarceration." It is a system that "brands people, often at very young ages, as 'criminals' and then ushers them into a parallel universe in which they may be denied the right to vote and be subject to legal discrimination in employment, housing, and basic public benefits for the rest of their lives." (Alexander 2020, xxvii)

The following passage from her book, while not surprising, is nonetheless stunning. "Those who define 'mass incarceration' narrowly, to include only currently locked in prisons or jails, erase from public view the overwhelming majority of people ensnared by the system. *Twice as many people are on probation or parole in this country as are locked in literal cages* (italics hers). The United States has a staggering 2.3 million people in prison—a higher rate of incarceration than any country in the world—but it also has another 4.5 million people under state control outside of prisons, on probation or parole. More than 70 million Americans—over twenty percent of the entire US population, overwhelmingly poor and disproportionately people of color—now have criminal records that authorize legal discrimination for life." P. xxviii

Those are staggering statistics. Alexander calls out a mistake I have made and am certain most Whites have also made, specifically, that "it is a mistake to think of mass incarceration as simply a problem of too many people in prisons and jails. It is that, but it is also much, much more. Prison statistics barely begin to capture the enormity of this crisis. And yet for too many, the discussion begins and ends there." (Alexander 2020, xxix)

Here's a case in point regarding how White dudes, myself included, have sought to end that debate, and thus shield ourselves from the horrifying realities of mass incarceration and its impact on people and communities of color. We say, "Well, according to the statistics, over half of those in prisons have committed violent criminal acts. This is about keeping people safe."

I had always accepted this statistic because it is technically true. But it is wildly misleading. It's such a powerful, insightful, and critical concept to understand that I will quote her at length. This point is simply too important to do otherwise.

"[T]he fact that half of a state's prison population is comprised of people labeled violent offenders does *not* mean that half of the people sentenced to prison in that state have been convicted of violent crimes. This may seem confusing or counterintuitive at first, but if you pause to consider how the system actually operates, this fact becomes obvious. People who are convicted of violent crimes tend to get longer prison sentences than those who commit nonviolent offenses. As a result, people who are classified as violent offenders comprise a much larger share of the prison population than they would if they had shorter sentences." (Alexander 2020, xxiv – xxv)

She explains further:

"Picture in your mind a prison hallway lined with cells (ten on each side) that are occupied by people for varying lengths of time. Imagine that each cell holds two people. One side of the hallway is reserved for people who have been convicted of drug or property crimes and who have relatively short sentences of five years or fewer. The other side of the hallway is reserved for people who have been convicted of violent crimes and sentenced to long mandatory minimums (ten years or more) or life imprisonment. During a single decade, more than a hundred people could cycle in and out of the cages reserved for those convicted of nonviolent crimes, while the same twenty people who are locked up for violent crimes on the other side of the hallway would remain in place. At any given moment, if you were to snap a picture of that hallway, half of the people living in cages would be classified as '*violent offenders*.' But this picture would wildly distort your understanding of the population who had been sentenced to prison during the past ten years. Although prison hallways are not segregated in this fashion, some version of this dynamic occurs in prisons across America, resulting in prisons that are half full of people convicted of violent crimes, even though most people sentenced to prisons and jails have been convicted of lesser offenses." (Alexander 2020, xxv)

That clear and concise explanation of how our system of mass incarceration operates jolted my understanding and knowledge base regarding how government sponsored policies and the war on drugs have contributed to our severe case of systemic racism. Slavery and Jim

Crow laws and practices were about maintaining control over Black folk, and so is our system of mass incarceration. It's slavery of another sort.

Need more proof? Here's what Alexander writes about the percentage of Blacks who have been incarcerated for drug crimes versus Whites. "Human Rights watch reported in 2000 that, in seven states, African Americans constitute 80 to 90 percent of all those sent to prison on drug charges. In at least fifteen states, Blacks are admitted to prison on drug charges at a rate of twenty to fifty-seven times greater than White men. In fact, nationwide, the rate of incarceration for African Americans convicted of drug offenses dwarfs the rate of whites." (Alexander 2020, 122, 123)

This, despite the well-established fact that most illegal drug users and dealers are White. Simply accepting those numbers as gospel truth has allowed us to justify our indifference to the realities of the US criminal justice system and mass incarceration.

It is a system that must change. And it is a system that us Old White Dudes need to acknowledge, become more educated about, accept our responsibility for and finally, to act in some way, to be a part of changing it. Even if it's as simple as informing friends and family about how the system works and challenging them to do the same or perhaps donating to the NAACP, which does good work in this space. In other words, it's time to do something.

As mentioned, the journey I refer to in this book is actually two journeys, my personal journey and MFE's journey and evolution as an organization. Here's an example of how Alexander's book caused us to rethink some aspects of our Songs For Justice project. Recall that the original concept was that each volume in the series of records would identify a group of people, whether Black, Hispanic/Latino, immigrant, or LGBTQ+, highlighting various issues relating to justice and equity that applied to those groups. But achieving a better understanding of how corrupt and discriminatory the system of mass incarceration compelled us to do a record that highlighted criminal justice reform. This is another example of how we are doing more than simply talking about justice. We are leveraging our resources to take direct action.

For those who continue to believe we are in a *post-racial* world, or that twice electing a Black president means we live in a colorblind society, please consider the negative impact of our criminal justice and mass incarceration system on Black Americans. It is profound and should give you pause or at least challenge you to reconsider perceptions about race, justice, and equity in America.

# CHAPTER ELEVEN

# ISSUES ON THE TABLE

*"Life's piano can only produce the melodies of brotherhood when it is recognized that the black keys are as basic, necessary and beautiful as the white keys"*

—Martin Luther King, Jr.

Everyone has signature events in their lifetimes, events that provoke significant change in yourself, the world . . . or both, events that change your outlook, challenge your beliefs, or occur out of nowhere to turn your world upside down. Maybe a serious health scare, winning the lottery, or meeting someone who influences you in a life changing manner. We've all had them (although I am still waiting for that life changing lottery ticket). George Floyd's murder and the civil unrest that followed was one for me.

The Floyd tragedy made me realize that as much as I have tried to be a force against racism, I needed to do more. Fortunately, MFE provided a vehicle for that to happen through the Songs For Justice record series. While it allowed me to act on my convictions in a concrete and meaningful way, I wanted more. Hence, the idea for this book was born.

It's been a journey of deep reflection and hard realizations. It has required a lot of work and a lot of time. I've read and continue to read just about anything I can get my hands on regarding these issues. Over the past three years, I have been thinking constantly about how to continue to learn, evolve, and become a more effective force for social justice.

It is also gratifying to make a commitment to do something important, to step into the abyss and open yourself up to the possibility that perhaps you might be able to influence or inspire someone else to do the same. That possibility, no matter how small, is liberating.

I have learned that there are so many more things related to these issues I don't fully understand. The more I learn, the more there is to learn. There are so many elements, angles, layers, and perspectives around these issues—and no easy answers.

Consider chapters twelve through thirty-eight that follow an "Issues Grab Bag," or if we were playing Jeopardy, answering questions from the "Anything Goes" category. What follows are short chapters in which I offer observations, impressions, and questions regarding various issues, debates, and theories that have reoccurred in my reading and research. They are addressed in no particular order, and my understanding of them is mixed. On some I feel well-informed and comfortable offering an opinion. On others, I'm still developing a more informed perspective. And there are some that I have far more questions than answers.

Some of my observations or opinions may not ring true to you. They are but one person's perspective. And because I am committed to continuous learning, feel free to disagree or correct me where I may be mistaken. Honest, thoughtful, criticism and debate are welcome. That's the way we all learn.

And that's the point.

# CHAPTER TWELVE

# SILENCE IS NO LONGER AN OPTION

*"To go against the dominant thinking of your friends, of most of the people you see every day, is perhaps the most difficult act of heroism you can perform"*

—Theodore H. White

Being a force against racism is not about charity. It's not about coming to the *rescue* of a beleaguered group. It's not about trying to make us feel good about ourselves or soothing our guilt. And, at the end of the day, it's not about people of color. It's about us Old White Dudes.

White men wrote our nation's foundational principles. And when they did, they codified White privilege or more specifically, White male privilege. Consider who wrote those founding documents. There were fifty-six signers of the Declaration of Independence, which, as we were taught in grade school reads in part, "We hold these truths to be self-evident, that all men are created equal, that they are endowed by their Creator with certain unalienable Rights, that among these are Life, Liberty, and the pursuit of Happiness."

Note that of the fifty-six white signers the majority—forty-one—were enslavers. In the minds of our Founding Fathers, only *White men* were created equal. Black men and all women were not worthy of those same unalienable rights.

From that original seed evolved a system designed to preserve and defend that privilege, often at any cost. The system is stacked against the achievement of equity because, to this day, Old White Dudes dominate our system of government. Take for example, the US Senate. In the history of that body, there have only been eleven

Black senators. Today that number is three of 100. And since the US Supreme Court was established in 1789, 108 out of the total of 116 justices have been White men.

Yes, we have made progress with Barack Obama being elected president twice and now with Kamala Harris as vice president. But the overall numbers do not lie. That's why it's no surprise we are seeing a rash of bills at the state level designed to limit voting access and suppress voter turnout, primarily among people of color. This is another means by which the White male dominated establishment maintains White privilege and power.

Again, I understand that you haven't *done anything* overtly and purposefully racist. But that does not excuse you from not *doing something* to mitigate its negative impact. We have been complicit in our silence and inaction. Doing nothing is an act in and of itself—an act of omission. We've been complicit in not standing up and accepting personal responsibility to work at dismantling a system of White privilege from which we have benefitted. This is about our core being as humans. It's about taking responsibility to work to right a wrong. It's about first healing ourselves. And a first step is to look in the mirror and acknowledge that White privilege is real. And then we've got to step up and do the hard work. We can do better. It's like that cartoon where Pogo looks into the mirror and sees that "the enemy is us."

"We cannot change the hypocrisy upon which we were founded," writes Nikole Hannah-Jones in *The 1619 Project.* "We cannot change all the times in the past when this nation had the opportunity to do the right thing and chose to return to its basest inclinations. We cannot make up for all the lives lost and dreams snatched, for all the suffering endured. But we can atone for it. We can acknowledge the crime. And we can do something to set things right, to ease the hardship and hurt of so many of our fellow Americans. . . . None of us can be held responsible for the wrongs of our ancestors. But if today we choose not to do the right and necessary thing, *that* burden we own." (Hannah-Jones 2021, 475)

She continues, "[W]e must make a choice about which America we want to build for tomorrow. The time for slogans and symbolism and inconsequential actions has long passed. Citizens inherited not just the glory of their nation but its wrongs too. A truly great country does not ignore or excuse its sins. It confronts them, and then works to make them right.

"If we are to be redeemed, we must do what is just: we must finally, live up to the magnificent ideals upon which we were founded." (Hannah-Jones 20212, 476)

Sometimes it is less about what you do or say than what you didn't say or do. The times you didn't step up or do something are the times that haunt you. Why didn't I say something? Why didn't I speak up, step up, or do something?

In some ways, the struggle for racial justice is like grass roots, guerilla warfare—family to family, friend to friend, neighbor to neighbor, block by block, and community by community. Like a rock thrown into a pond that sends ripples in all directions, your voice can similarly echo. If you show the courage to say or do something, there will be others who, because of your courage and actions, will also step up. Many people who want to do the right thing simply need a bit of inspiration to take that first step. In stepping up first, you provide cover and give them an example to follow.

In short, it is not enough simply to deny being racist. Rather, we should actively denounce or oppose various racist notions, regardless of how widely believed. Racist words, slurs, slogans, memes, and beliefs must be actively challenged and called out. Repeatedly. Not stepping up to say something says an awful lot. Silence is complicity. Which means silence is no longer an option.

# CHAPTER THIRTEEN

## RACE AS A SOCIAL CONSTRUCT

*"Race is the child of racism, not the father."*

—Ta-Nehisi Coates

According to Merriam-Webster, a social construct is an idea that has been created and accepted by the people in a society. In other words, they are shared ideas or perceptions that exist only because people in a group or society choose to accept them. Or, to put a finer point on it, social constructs are created out of thin air. They are fabricated and promoted to such a degree that a segment of society accepts them as having meaning, or as truth. For example, the idea that pink is for girls and blue is for boys is an example of a social construct related to gender. There is, however, no data or scientific research to support that belief.

Race is a social construct. It is a system of stratification based on the belief that some racial groups are superior to other racial groups.

Anthropology and human evolutionary biology prove that all humans are of the same type, species, and kind. Research shows a lack of genetic difference between racial groups. In other words, the difference between Whites and Blacks is literally skin deep. Under the skin, we are no different. We're essentially genetically identical. Yet, why is the notion of the racial inferiority of POC so prevalent?

Historically, creating human hierarchies around constructs such as race, ethnicity, or groups did not originate in America. It is traceable to Aristotle. Ibrahm X. Kendhi references this in his work *Stamped From the Beginning: The Definitive History of Racist Ideas in America.* He writes:

"In studying Aristotle's philosophy, Puritans learned rationales for human hierarchy, and they began to believe that some groups were superior to other groups. In Aristotle's case, ancient Greeks were superior to all non-Greeks. But Puritans believed they were superior to Native Americans, the African people, and even Anglicans—that is all non-Puritans. Aristotle, who lived from 384 to 322 BCE, concocted a climate theory to justify Greek superiority, saying that extreme hot or cold climates produced intellectually, physically, and morally inferior people who were ugly and lacked the capacity for freedom and self-government. . . . All of this was in the interest of normalizing Greek slaveholding practices and Greece's rule over the western Mediterranean. . . . Humanity is divided into two: the masters and the slaves, or, if one prefers it, the Greeks and the Barbarians, those who have the right to command; and those who are born to obey." (Kendhi 2016, 17)

While the human hierarchy social construct did not originate in America, it took hold in White society when the first enslaved Africans arrived on our shores in 1619. It was there that the concept got repurposed for New World Whites, who promoted and perpetuated the narrative about Black inferiority to placate their guilt for their unjust and utterly cruel treatment of Black people.

Robin DiAngelo explains. "Freedom and equality—regardless of religion or class status—were radical new ideas when the United States was formed. At the same time, the US economy was based on the abduction and enslavement of African people, the displacement and genocide of Indigenous people and the annexation of Mexican lands. . . . The tension between the noble ideology of equality and the reality of genocide, enslavement and colonization had to be reconciled. . . . The idea of racial inferiority was created to justify unequal treatment; belief in racial inferiority is not what triggered unequal treatment." (DiAngelo 2018, 15 & 16)

The most powerful passage I've read about race being a social construct comes from Lillian Smith, considered by many the foremost White liberal writer of the mid-twentieth century. Her book *Killers of the Dream*, first published in 1978, is one of the most powerful critiques of the pre-1960's American South. Here's what she wrote:

"Hypocrisy, greed, self-righteousness, defensiveness twisted in men's minds. The South grew more sensitive to criticism, more defensive and dishonest in its thinking. For deep down in their hearts, southerners knew they were wrong. They knew it in slavery as they later knew that sharecropping was wrong, and as they know now that segregation is wrong. . . . Our grandparents called themselves Christians and sometimes believed they were. Believing it, they were compelled to believe it was morally right for them to hold slaves. They could not say, 'We shall keep our slaves because they are profitable, regardless of right and wrong.'" (Smith 1949, 1961, 61)

And this is where it gets very interesting as she essentially implies that Southerners used the excuse that God allowed them to enslave Black people.

"Our grandfathers' conscience compelled them to justify slavery and they did; by making the black man 'different', setting him outside God's law, reducing him to less than human . . . they took God's place and 'decided' which of His creatures have souls and which do not. And once doing it, they continued doing it, and their sons continued doing it, and their grandsons, telling themselves and their children more and more and more lies about white superiority until they no longer knew the truth and were lost in a maze of fantasy and falsehood that had little resemblance to the actual world they lived in." (Smith 1949, 1961, 61)

At risk of oversimplifying, as a nation we couldn't square our supposed fundamental principles of Christianity and America's promise of all men being created equal, not to mention women, when we were enslaving Blacks. The White powers that be had to devise a theory or proof to justify the enslavement, cruel treatment, and exploitation of Blacks. Touting them as "inferior" became the construct. Eventually, enough White folks, including political and business leaders as well as some scientists, developed and promoted this notion of inferiority, and it became, at least in the White world, accepted as fact.

"The beneficiaries of slavery, segregation and mass incarceration have produced racist ideas of Black people being best suited for or deserving of the confines of slavery, segregation, or the jail cell", adds Ibrahm X. Kendi in *Stamped from the Beginning*. "Consumers of these racist ideas have been led to believe there is something wrong with Black people, and not the policies that have enslaved, oppressed, and confined so many Black people." (Kendhi 2016, 10)

In other words, it's not Black *people*, who are responsible for the inequalities and the negative life consequences and outcomes that result from those inequalities. Rather, *policies* lead to such social, economic, and health disparities. And here's the rub as Kendi sees it. If we in fact believe, as our Constitution suggests, that we are all created equal, then the wide disparity in the conditions can only be the result of systemic discrimination.

In his book *Tears We Cannot Stop: A Sermon to White America*, Michael Eric Dyson puts it this way: "After more than a century of enlightened study, we know that race is not just something that falls from the sky, it is, as anthropologists say, a fabricated idea. But that doesn't mean that race doesn't have material consequences and empirical weight. It simply means that if we constructed it, we can get about the business of deconstructing it." (Dyson 2017, 2021, 67)

If we can concoct a social construct around racial inferiority, we can also create, promote, and perpetuate an alternative social construct around justice and equity for all, including Black Americans. That will take a lot of work. The question is whether we are willing to do the work necessary to create and perpetuate that alternative construct.

# CHAPTER FOURTEEN

## EQUALITY VS. EQUITY

*"Justice that is not rooted in equity, in social welfare and in community, is not justice at all."*

—Deray McKesson

Kevin Ressler is a friend and active social justice advocate in addition to his job as executive director of the United Way of Lancaster. He was the first person I asked to read the Introduction to this book. It took him exactly two sentences before he looked at me and said, "Damn, you already sound like an Old White Dude!"

"What are you talking about?" I asked.

"Equality versus equity," he stated. "While equality has been used forever, a more accurate and contemporary descriptor is equity." He patiently explained the important difference between the two.

While both terms promote fairness and are often used interchangeably, there is an important distinction. *Equality* means that each individual or group is given the same resources and opportunities and that a suitable outcome is achieved by treating everyone the same, regardless of need or history of access and opportunity.

Meanwhile, *equity*, the term used in this book, achieves fairness through treating people differently depending on their need. Equity recognizes that each person has different circumstances, thus the allocation of resources and opportunities needed to mitigate those differences to reach an equal outcome are varied.

He offered this example. Two people, one tall, the other short, while standing, are attempting to watch a baseball game being played on the other side of a solid fence. Providing both the same sized crate to stand on to see over the fence represents an equal solution. However, because of the height discrepancy, the crate might be high enough to allow the tall person to see over the fence but not the short person. While the proposed solution provided an equal opportunity, it did not achieve an outcome that results in equality. An equitable solution would recognize the difference in height and thus provide the shorter person a taller box.

His point was that the historical discrimination against Black Americans and the resultant inequities must be considered when addressing mitigation measures. To think that providing access to a service based on a solution applied in an equal fashion will result in an equal outcome does not recognize the vastly different social, educational, financial, and related circumstances that POC face. To achieve equality requires that those different circumstances be recognized and incorporated into the proposed solutions.

This lesson reinforced the larger issue of how language around racial justice issues has become so nuanced. Further, it brought home how providing the same resources and opportunities does not make up for historical systemic disadvantages. While there are only two additional letters needed to transform equity into equality, in this context, equality and equity are fundamentally different.

Thank you, Kevin Ressler.

# CHAPTER FIFTEEN

## BORN ON THIRD BASE

*"I hate the unfairness of injustice. Anyone who thinks they are better than others or 'chosen' or feel they have entitlement . . . be it through monarchy, government, or money. I think we are all born the same. We are entitled to an equal shot at life."*

—Liam Cunningham

One of the major roadblocks in the ability of White folks, particularly, White males, to accept the notion of social justice for all is the inability to recognize that many of us were born on third base thinking we hit a triple.

It begins with the American ideal that anyone who works hard enough can make it. Yes, working hard increases chances of success, financial or otherwise. And I understand the tendency to take pride in having earned everything you've achieved without handouts. We all like to think we have overcome adversity and achieved success because of effort and virtue rather than privilege and some luck. The flip side is that someone who is struggling or poor or perhaps gets in trouble with the law *deserves* it because he or she is lazy, not smart, or flawed in some way.

"I made it. Why can't they? If I can do it why can't they?"

An important first step in becoming a positive force for social justice is to recognize that for Black folk, systemic racism has littered the path to success and making it with obstacle upon obstacle. That's why virtually every Black parent must tell their children they will have to perform twice as good as White folk to get or keep a job. This should not be surprising. After all, we're talking about a country that had written into its founding document that Blacks were counted as three-fifths of a person.

In response, it is common to invoke false comparisons between Blacks and other immigrant groups such as Italians, Jews, and the Irish. The claim that these groups had similar challenges but made it nonetheless does not tell the entire story. Once again, let's leave it to Martin Luther King to set the record straight. He wrote in *Where Do We Go From Here: Community or Chaos*,

"Why haven't the Negroes done the same? These questioners refuse to see that the situation of other immigrant groups a hundred years ago and the situation of the Negro today cannot be usefully compared. Negroes were brought here in chains long before the Irish decided *voluntarily* to leave Ireland, or the Italians thought of leaving Italy. Some Jews may have left their homes in Europe involuntarily, but they were not in chains when they arrived on these shores. Other immigrant groups came to America with language and economic handicap, but not with the stigma of color. Above all, no other ethnic group has been a slave on American soil, and no other group has had its family structure deliberately torn apart. That is the rub." (King 1968, 110)

My typical response when I hear an Old White Dude suggest he is a success due to his hard work and that everyone else can achieve such success if they only worked as hard, goes something like this. "So, the fact that you grew up in a stable household without having to worry about having adequate food or healthcare didn't give you an advantage? Or that you attended a well-funded, often private, school and had parents who could pay for you to go to a good college? Or that when you began your career, you were able to get your foot in the door because your parents or their friends had contacts to open those doors of opportunity. Or maybe you were able to take an entry level, unpaid internship because your parents were able to support you while others couldn't take advantage of such an opportunity because they had to work to help the family pay the rent."

Their response often goes something like this. "Today everyone has the same rights, by law. Everyone is equal. In fact, with today's affirmative action measures, it's the White man who is being denied equal opportunity. How can you say systemic racism is a problem today? We elected a Black president twice and now have vice president of Jamaican and Indian descent."

Yes, we have made progress in becoming a more just society. But over 400 years of discrimination against Black folk throughout virtually every facet of American life cannot be erased with the passage of a few laws and election results brought into line within a generation. From health care to housing, from the education system to the legal system, from policing to the prison system, from voting rights to access to capital, the myriad of hurdles to advancement for Black Americans are formidable and, in many cases, overwhelming. Such a deeply ingrained system will take tens of decades to fully transform. It will be a long and difficult path. But it's a path that we all must pursue in doing the tough work to undo systemic racism at its core.

The All-American notion of the rugged individualist who succeeds due to superior talent, intellect, and work ethic is an enduring mythology of the American experience. It's an easy narrative to embrace when it comes to social justice because it essentially provides an excuse to justify White privilege. It lets us off the hook for taking responsibility to understand the root causes of injustice and inequity. It also tends to cloud our judgement regarding exactly how much we benefit from White privilege. We've got to acknowledge reality as it is, not how we imagine it to be.

In other words, you may be standing on third base, but you definitely did not hit a triple. And there is absolutely no shame in admitting that.

# CHAPTER SIXTEEN

## THE GOOD OLD DAYS?

*"Nothing is more responsible for the good old days than a bad memory."*
—Franklin Pierce Adams

I am no political scientist, but I do know that people vote for candidates for complex and varied reasons. Regardless, the polling numbers and demographics around Donald Trump's "Make America Great Again" (MAGA) message in the 2016 Presidential campaign resonated with a lot of people, mostly White, and in particular White males. Trump espoused that as a country, we need to get back to the good old days. His campaign rhetoric focused on turning back the hands of time to a "greater" time and a "greater" America.

But when exactly, and for whom, was America a greater country? Clearly, our country has always been "great" for White dudes. After all, we have been writing the rules forever. But what about everyone else? For everyone else, America has not necessarily been all that great.

My perspective about the not-so-great good old days was expanded by Robin DiAngelo in her wonderful book, *White Fragility: Why it's so Hard for White People to Talk About Racism*. In fact, the extent to which she documents just how *not* so good the good old days were is profound. She writes:

"As a white person, I can openly and unabashedly reminisce about "the good old days". Romanticized recollections of the past and calls for a return to former ways are a function of white privilege, which manifests itself in the ability to remain oblivious to our racial history. Claiming that the past was socially better than the present is also a hallmark of white supremacy. Consider any period in the past from the perspective of people of color: 246 years of brutal enslavement; the rape of black women for the pleasure of white men and to produce more enslaved workers; the selling off of black children; the attempted genocide of Indigenous people; Indian removal acts and reservations; indentured servitude, lynching and mob violence; sharecropping; Chinese exclusion laws; Japanese American internment; Jim Crow laws of mandatory segregation; black codes; bans on black jury service; bans on voting; imprisoning people for unpaid work; medical sterilization and experimentation; employment discrimination; educational discrimination; inferior schools; biased laws and policing practices; redlining and subprime mortgages; mass incarceration; racist media representations; cultural erasures; attacks, and mockery; and untold and perverted historical accounts, and you can see how a romanticized past is strictly a white construct. But it is a powerful construct because it calls out to a deeply internalized sense of superiority and entitlement and the sense that any advancement for people of color is an encroachment on this entitlement." (DiAngelo 2018, 59)

The "good old days"? I had to re-read that paragraph three times to fully grasp its scope.

This is another example of why we need to do the work of reading and researching regarding our past. It is why we need to be honest and face the truth because if we do not, we are bound to regress into a past that was, for pretty much everyone other than White men, not so great.

In fact, in some ways, we have been taking a few steps back with various restrictions being put in place to make it harder for people, particularly POC, to vote, and certainly with the recent Supreme Court decision to overturn Roe V. Wade. Do we really want to march backwards? If that is the case, then where do we stop? Do we march backwards to a reconstituted age of Jim Crow? Or a world where women were less than full citizens?

Yes, there are some things that I wish could be rolled back to a simpler, less frantic, and confusing age. For example, I wouldn't mind returning to a world where social media didn't rule our lives. But issues relating to social justice and human rights? No way! There is only one direction to march regarding social justice and human rights and that is *forward* with the destination being equality for all.

In other words, maybe the old days were pretty good for us Old White Dudes. But for virtually everyone else? Not so much.

# CHAPTER SEVENTEEN

# EXHAUSTION

*"I'm sick and tired of being sick and tired."*

—Fannie Lou Hamer

As mentioned in the Preface, it's hard to imagine how exhausting it must be to be Black in America. Black folk have had to deal with hate and discrimination twenty-four hours a day, seven days a week, 365 days a year for over 400 years. The sheer enormity of their suffering in seeking acknowledgment and recognition as equal human beings, measured over that timeline, is stunning.

Martin Luther King, in his final book before his assassination, *Where Do We Go From Here: Chaos or Community?* offers a passage that places the enormity of the struggles of Black Americans into a broader context.

"For years the Negro has been taught that he is nobody, that his color is a sign of his biological depravity, that his being has been stamped with the indelible imprint of inferiority, that his whole history has been soiled with the filth of worthlessness. All too few people realize how slavery and racial segregation have scarred the soul and wounded the spirit of the black man. The whole dirty business of slavery was based on the premise that the Negro was a thing to be used, not a person to be respected." (King 1968, 39)

As OWDs, we might think we know and appreciate the extent of Black America's struggle for justice. But when you begin to uncover the history, hear the stories, see the pictures, and listen to the songs, you realize it is far more sordid, cruel, and heartbreaking than you could ever have imagined. You can't fully understand the extent of the suffering unless you do the work of educating yourself, peering under all the historical rocks. And the saddest part is that the driving force behind all of it is not true. It's based on a false social construct.

The challenges for Black Americans in navigating our White world daily is something of which we have little understanding. The extent of the stress in having to do so is beyond anything I'd ever imagined. Consider this passage from an essay by Linda Villarosa, in *The 1619 Project*, which introduced the term "weathering," the reality for Blacks in America, as she explored how even Blacks with adequate health care are more vulnerable to incur serious diseases, "[T]hey are affected by the stress of coping with racism embedded in day-to-day life, which can lead to a kind of premature aging. Arline T. Geronimus, a professor at the University of Michigan School of Public Health, does research in this area; she coined the term 'weathering' to explain how high-effort coping in the face of continuous racial insults exacts a physical price on bodies of Black Americans." (Hannah-Jones 2021, 317)

That is something many White folks do not understand. At all. I certainly didn't. The least we can do is to acknowledge the enormity of it.

For us to move forward on our individual journeys to become a positive force for justice requires empathy in understanding the realities of the Black experience in America. "What is needed today on the part of white America is a committed altruism . . . True altruism is more than the capacity to pity; it is the capacity to empathize." wrote Martin Luther King, Jr. in *Where Do We Go from Here: Chaos or Community?* "Pity is feeling sorry for someone; empathy is feeling sorry with someone. Empathy is fellow feeling for the person in need—his pain, agony and burdens. I doubt if the problems of our teeming ghettos will have a great chance to be solved until the white majority, through genuine empathy, comes to feel the ache and anguish of the Negroes' daily life." (King 1968, 107)

As mentioned, my basketball experiences often placed me in situations where I was in the minority and thus did not control the general mores and team culture. I got a very small taste of those challenges. But even then, once outside the locker room, I lived in a world where dudes who looked like me made all the rules.

That, compared to the 24/7/365/400+ year reality that Blacks have had to face? Given that history, how can you downplay or deny the ongoing struggle of Black Americans for justice and equity? Rather, we should be saluting the sheer courage, utter determination, sharp intelligence, and devoted loyalty needed to survive such relentless challenges. And despite all of that, still having the faith to continue to believe in America. It's not only breathtaking, but also inspiring.

It is time for us Old White Dudes to place our White fragility in our back pockets and acknowledge some truths. While that may be uncomfortable, it is nothing to fear. The advancement of Black folk, whether educationally, economically, socially, or otherwise is not an encroachment on our White privilege. The fact is, when our neighbors are healthier, better educated, have a solid roof over their heads, and more nutritious food on the table, we all benefit. When our neighbors and fellow citizens are doing better, so are we. This is not a zero-sum game.

Let's be honest. Being Black in the United States is exhausting. In the words of Ed Tapscott, former college basketball coach and the first Black CEO of an NBA franchise, "Every Black man wakes up in the morning with two jobs—his job and being a Black man." (Feinstein pg. 235)

How do you think you would feel if you had to face such relentless challenges 24/7/365?

I'd imagine that you too, would be exhausted.

# CHAPTER EIGHTEEN

# COLOR-BLINDNESS

*"We would like to get to a point in our society where people really
are color blind and this message would not have to be told anymore.
Unfortunately, we're not there yet."*

—Harry Connick, Jr.

How often have you heard someone claim to be "color blind"?
I've always been uncomfortable with this notion. While the
intent is understandable and noble, how can you NOT notice someone's
skin color? It's the first thing you see when you meet someone. Still,
it never occurred to me that saying and believing you are color blind
can be harmful.

Most scholars agree that when it comes to race there is no such
thing as color blindness. The following are observations from select
writers, such as Michelle Alexander, Heather McGhee, and Cornel
West.

Alexander writes, "[T]o aspire to colorblindness is to aspire to a
state of being in which you are not capable of seeing racial difference—a
practical impossibility for most of us . . . The colorblindness ideal is
premised on the notion that as a society we can never be trusted to
see race and treat each other fairly or with genuine compassion. A
commitment to color consciousness, by contrast, places faith in our
capacity as humans to show care and concern for others, even as we
are fully cognizant of race and possible racial differences . . . It is easier
to imagine a world in which we tolerate racial differences by being
blind to them.

"The uncomfortable truth, however, is that racial differences will *always* exist among us. Even if the legacies of slavery, Jim Crow and mass incarceration were completely overcome, we would remain a nation of immigrants (and indigenous people) in a larger world divided by race and ethnicity . . . For the foreseeable future, racial and ethnic inequality will be a feature of American life." (Alexander 2020, 302, 303)

Alexander crystallized my thinking on why it never made sense how people could claim to be colorblind. But her next point was an "aha!" moment. She assures us that while we may never reach a total, idealistic world of perfect racial equality, it is not a cause for alarm or despair. She goes on to point out the danger in such thinking.

"What is concerning is the real possibility that we, as a society, will choose not to care. We will choose to be blind to injustice and the suffering of others. We will look the other way and deny our public agencies the resources, data, and tools they need to solve problems. We will refuse to celebrate what is beautiful about our distinct cultures and histories even as we blend and evolve. That is cause for despair."

"Seeing race is not the problem. Refusing to care for the people we see is the problem. The fact that the meaning of race may evolve over time or lose much of its significance is hardly a reason to be struck blind. We should hope not for a colorblind society but instead for a world in which we can see each other fully, learn from each other, and do what we can to respond to each other with love. That was King's dream—a society that is capable of seeing each of us, as we are, with love. That is a goal worth fighting for." (Alexander 2020, 303)

This leads to a point made by Heather McGhee in, *The Sum of Us*. McGhee writes that claiming to be color blind dismisses or denies that racism exists. In other words, it provides another excuse for Whites not to accept accountability and responsibility to learn and grow in terms of how we view and treat people of other races.

She writes, "Color blindness has become a powerful weapon against progress for people of color, but as a denial mindset, it doesn't do white people any favors, either. A person who avoids the realities of racism doesn't build the crucial muscles for navigating cross-cultural tensions or recovering with grace from missteps. That person is less likely to listen deeply to unexpected ideas expressed by people from other cultures or to do the research on her own to learn about her blind spots. When that person then faces the inevitable uncomfortable racial reality—an offended co-worker, a presentation about racial disparity at a PTA meeting, her inadvertent use of a stereotype—she's caught flat-footed. Denial leaves people ill-prepared to function or thrive in a diverse society." (McGhee 2021, 230)

Cornell West, philosopher, political activist, social critic, and public intellectual, writes in his foreword to *The New Jim Crow*, "Martin Luther King Jr. called on us to be lovestruck with each other, not colorblind toward each other. To be lovestruck is to care, to have deep compassion, and to be concerned for each and every individual, including the poor and the vulnerable." (Alexander 2020, xlix)

In short, we need to see, accept, and love each other. If we are ever going to begin to work on building bridges between differences, we must first acknowledge the need to build them. Not only should we stop claiming to be color blind, but we should also think about why it is that we should ditch the term and notion behind it. The fact is, no one is color blind when it comes to race. Claiming otherwise, while well intended, is disingenuous and counterproductive. In other words, it's okay to admit to the fact that you do see color. The question, however, is once acknowledged, what are you going to do to mitigate the impacts that have resulted from that false notion?

# CHAPTER NINETEEN

## DIVERSITY EQUALS MATURITY AND STRENGTH

*"It is not our differences that divide us. It is our inability to recognize,*
*accept and celebrate those differences."*

—Audre Lorde

Good sports coaches understand that maximum success requires leveraging and utilizing the full range of talents of every player. Each player has a unique skill set. The challenge is to recognize, analyze, encourage, develop, and utilize that broad set of talents for maximum team results.

This principle was reinforced by one of my coaches at Davidson, Dave Pritchett. He often spoke of coaching the team "from the thirteenth player up." He paid more attention to the last guy on the bench than he did the best player. He understood that to maximize team performance, each team member was essential, regardless of how much playing time they received.

I had a unique view of this principle. As mentioned, my oldest brother, Greg, also played basketball at Davidson. While I was considered the team's best player, Greg was the last guy on the bench. We both contributed to our team, albeit in different, unique ways. Regardless, we both loved playing basketball for Davidson. Greg's experience gave me an appreciation for how every player on a team or every employee of a company has an important role to play and that maximizing team or company performance depends on everyone fulfilling their individual roles to the best of their ability.

It's like a tasty Louisiana gumbo. You are not going to create a good, thick, spicy gumbo using only two ingredients. Gumbo requires many spices complimenting each other and coming together to create a great taste. Another example is your neighborhood. A broad cross section of people, with different interests, backgrounds, and talents, makes for a more interesting and dynamic neighborhood. As with a basketball team, gumbo, a business, non-profit organization, neighborhood, community, or country, a diverse whole is greater than the sum of its parts.

In *The Sum of Us*, Heather McGhee cites research from Dr. Katherine W. Phillips of Columbia Business School that strongly suggests that diversity results in better group decision making and outcomes. She reported, "Being with similar others leads us to think we all hold the same information and share the same perspective. This perspective, which stopped all white groups from effectively processing the information is what hinders creativity and innovation." (McGhee 2021, 281)

McGhee sums this point up well. "Put simply, we need each other. Our differences have the potential to make us stronger, smarter, more creative, and fairer. Once we abandon the false idea of zero-sum competition, the benefits of diversity become evident, from the classroom to the courtroom to the boardroom." (McGhee 2021, 281)

This makes sense. If you spend all your time with people who look like you, and have had similar life experiences and thus, tend to think like you, your potential for growth, whether personal or as a business, will be limited. If you surround yourself with like-minded people, you are not as likely to be challenged in your beliefs or ideas and, as a result, have less opportunity to learn and grow. If everyone thinks the same way, the thinking of the collective will become narrow and ultimately ineffective in our increasingly complex and diverse economy, society, and world community. Not to mention how boring life would be if everyone were the same.

As Maya Angelou wrote, "It is time parents teach young people early on that in diversity, there is beauty, and there is strength."

# CHAPTER TWENTY

# CANCEL CULTURE

*"I try not to cancel people. But at some point, we got to stand up and say, hey, right is right, wrong is wrong."*

—Rex Chapman

B eing a force against racism involves risk. It requires lifting your head up out of the sand to confront your biases and shortcomings. It can be quite uncomfortable.

The prevalence of social media has increased those risks exponentially. The debate around race, equity, and social justice, while always challenging, has become increasingly raw and emotionally charged with much of that increased divisiveness fueled by social media. Those who have been discriminated against for centuries are far less patient with those who act in discriminatory ways. That is understandable. On the other hand, Whites are often gripped with fear of saying or doing something considered out of line or disrespectful, whether intentional or not, and being called out or canceled as a result. Social media has created an environment where canceling can be rapid and devastating.

But being called out isn't necessarily a bad thing if, as a result, you recognize and understand your mistakes and grow from them. By not being called out, you would likely misstate what you misstated, and as a result would continue to misstate it in the future. What is different after the Floyd murder is that people of color are increasingly calling out those mistakes. This is as it should be. It represents progress provided us OWDs are willing to listen and acknowledge our mistakes, learn from them, and grow in a positive way.

Despite a pure heart and genuine commitment to learn, I've made many mistakes or made disrespectful or not well thought out assumptions. When that happens, I expect to be called out. If being called out leads to an increased understanding of how my words or actions were out of line and caused others pain, I want to know about it. I don't want to repeat mistakes. For the most part, I've been fortunate in that those who have called me out were patient and generous in educating me regarding my errors. They have been gracious in providing space for redemption. Ideally, the result is using lessons learned to become an advocate for justice. The ability and opportunity to admit mistakes, take full responsibility for them, and use those lessons to teach others is powerful.

Those who are offended or feel they have been disrespected can post comments, complaints, and accusations on social media in real time. Such posts are often created in anger, more lashing out than thoughtful commentary. This is problematic because issues of race are nuanced and complex. With a few clicks of the keyboard, social media can increase the velocity and scope of an incident from a dead stop in Boise, Idaho, to a global audience in minutes. Or, as the saying goes, "Lies can travel around the world before the truth even gets its shoes on."

Given the complexity of these issues, they deserve not knee-jerk reactions but rather thoughtful consideration. Time and space should be considered allies as there is no hurry to comment or respond. It's helpful and smart to provide some time and space to sort through the situations and issues, allowing the nuances and complexities to be thoroughly and thoughtfully considered. Yes, people should be called out when appropriate, but people should also be provided some space to learn from mistakes.

One thing that was striking about the Black Lives Matter protests of 2020 is the large number of Whites who showed in the streets to march for social justice. Significant numbers of White folk believe and support the social justice issues at the center of the BLM movement. It is a positive development for so many to feel they can and should step up with a more active and visible role in these causes.

That said, stepping up can feel as if you are hunkered down in a fox hole on a field of war. While some may not consider war a good analogy, the fact is, our country has been and continues to be at "war" over issues of race.

At some point you raise your head out of the foxhole because you want to do your part in the fight. While you want to be a part of the solution, you've never spoken out or stepped forward on these issues. Because it is your first step, you might not be fully attuned to the nuances related to language and behavior. Regardless, you take a deep breath, raise your head, and commit to be a part of the solution. But sometimes after lifting your head out of the foxhole and, with no ill intent, you parse the wrong phrase or assume something that is off base. If, as a result, you are publicly scolded through social media, you may retreat into that foxhole, never to return to assume additional risks. As a result, a potential ally is lost.

Ultimately, when well-intended people who want to be a positive force for racial justice, make mistakes, we should provide them the space to assume accountability, learn, grow, and eventually become a more effective advocate and ally for the cause. No single act should define any of us. We should be judged by our life's body of work.

But why should trying to do the right thing scare you? If something is the right thing to do, you do it. If you believe in justice and equity, you should be willing to prove it with your actions rather than talking about it, even at the risk of making mistakes along the way.

And you do not take those actions and risks to get approval of the Black community. You do it because it's the right thing to do. As Tim Wise noted in *White Like Me: Reflections on Race from a Privileged Son*, "People of color don't owe us gratitude when we speak out against racism. They don't owe us a pat on the back. And if all they do is respond to our efforts with a terse 'it's about time,' that's fine. Challenging racism and white supremacy is what we *should* be doing. Resistance is what we need to do for *us*." (Wise 2008, 2011, 182)

Unfortunately, social media makes cancel culture easy. It's convenient to sit on a sofa surrounded by the comforts of home and tweet or post something to call out, unfriend, or cancel someone with whom you disagree. It is far easier to criticize or call out someone through social media than engage them in a thoughtful discussion where you can consider the nuances and education can occur.

Regardless of how you are called out, publicly or privately, the goal is not allowing your White fragility to prevent a thoughtful consideration of your mistakes to learn and do better in the future. In her book *Me and White Supremacy*, Layla F. Saad provides examples of reactions to getting called out that do not lead to growth and progress and improved personal responsibility.

My guess is that you have reacted in at least one, if not several, of the following ways when confronted with a challenging conversation regarding race and your biases. I know I have.

- "Becoming defensive, derailing, crying, falling silent, or dramatically leaving the space or conversation.
- Focusing on intent while ignoring or minimizing impact.
- Tone policing BIPOC by claiming you are being attacked or characterizing the person(s) calling you out as aggressive or irrational.
- Denying that your actions were racist because you do not see color (color blindness)
- Tokenizing BIPOC to prove you are not racist or talking about all the good things you have done for BIPOC (proving that these acts were actually optical allyship).
- Talking more than listening to the people calling you out/in.
- Focusing on how you can quickly fix things through optical allyship rather than really taking the time to reflect on your actions and do further research on what you are being called out/in for." (Saad 2020, 165 -166)

Saad goes on to address how the fear that many feel of being called out deters antiracism practice. "If you are constantly afraid of doing the wrong thing and being called out/in for it, then your antiracism work will easily slip into perfectionism, which will lead to:

- White fragility, because you have not built the resilience needed for doing this work.
- Tone policing, because you can only handle being called out/in if the message is delivered to you in a certain tone.
- White silence, because of the fear of saying the wrong thing.
- White exceptionalism, because you will continue to think that you are the exception to the rule, 'one of the good ones.'
- White apathy, because you will think 'What is the point if I am going to be called out/in.'
- Tokenism, because you will want a BIPOC to protect you from the pain of being called out/in.
- Optical allyship, because you will be more concerned with not being called out /in than with simply doing the work." (Saad, 2020, 167)

But here's the issue. As Saad writes, "There has been no safety for BIPOC under white supremacy. And the sense of perceived emotional danger that people with white privilege feel when being called out/in is so small when compared to what BIPOC experience through racism." (Saad 2020, 167)

If you are committed to learning, growing, and becoming a better ally, you will make mistakes. Thus, be prepared, at some point, to get called out. When you are, welcome it as a learning opportunity. It is all part of the work. There is no getting around it. It can be emotional and difficult. But it is necessary. This is not about you and your White privilege and fragility. It's about becoming more aware and sensitive about how your behavior can negatively impact others.

Wielding the cancel card is tricky. On one hand, it encourages people to listen more carefully and respectfully to each other, which advances the mission for a fair and more inclusive society. The flip side is shaming people online, particularly when comments are taken out of context, to push one's own agenda, can be counterproductive. In short, we White folk should be careful and humble in using the cancel card around issues of race.

Here's why.

Let's say someone posts something hurtful, misguided, or racist. It's easy to think that personally responding and piling on with criticism somehow makes you a courageous fighter for social justice. While racist statements or rants should be confronted and called out, social media is not an effective platform for making a real impact for two reasons. First, given the way Facebook uses its algorithms, when posting something, it is quite likely that the people who see and read it are, for the most part, people with whom you have a lot in common. That means you are likely preaching to the choir. The real impact of your posts is minimal at most; indeed, it could backfire and push the original poster away.

But here's the real drawback. It can give you a false sense of doing something meaningful around social justice. The satisfaction you might feel from the call out does not excuse you from doing the difficult self-examination of your own biases. It's easy to make a post supporting the Black Lives Matter movement from the comfort of the sofa in your living room and then sit back, feeling good about yourself, convinced you've done your part to make a difference. It's like simply posting a BLM sign in your yard or window. While that sort of public support is helpful, it has the potential for becoming an easy way to wash your hands of the issue. Making a periodic social media post has a minimal impact and does not challenge you in any real way to do something more meaningful.

Calling out or cancelling someone over an unintended racial gaffe is also tricky for another reason. Specifically, I am referring to calling out people being more about you than the real issues at hand. This is often referred to as "virtue signaling," which essentially means that your actions are more about telling others how virtuous you are rather than having and acting upon a real and personal commitment to social justice. That's why it is important to tread lightly in calling someone out, particularly if you are White. As such, you might want to ask yourself whether publicly calling out someone is the most effective way to have a real impact. While racial slights or gaffes should be called out, and doing so might make you feel superior and virtuous, the question is whether that is all you are going to do to advance justice and equity. Is that your entire game plan? Or is it more about self-aggrandizement as opposed to actually doing something concrete? In other words, you can't simply talk the talk and point fingers. If you want to have a real impact, you've got to do some real work and walk the walk.

While some may feel righteous in their efforts to call out or cancel someone, the reality is that social media platforms are not an effective vehicle to determine or mediate justice. They are mere platforms to voice opinions or outrage with little fact checking or moderating influence. As a result, once something is posted, it can quickly turn into a *mob rule* of people piling on rather than action that induces further understanding of issues. The challenge is how to strike a balance. As much as it is about Black and White, it's not black and white. It's complex and nuanced with many difficult and sensitive issues to navigate. And the fact is, no one has all the answers. That is why it is important we not cavalierly wield the cancel card.

# CHAPTER TWENTY-ONE

## ON RISK

*"He who is not courageous enough to take risks will accomplish nothing in life."*

—Muhammed Ali

**D**on't let risk paralyze you!

These are emotional and controversial issues. So, yes, there is plenty of risk to go around. Believe me, I get it. Been there, done that. I have felt the sting of being publicly called out and criticized for making an insenstive or clueless remark. But you can't let that paralyze you. If you know where your heart is and know your commitment to justice and equity, you must continue to move forward.

Jenee Desmond-Harris brilliantly wrote the following in an essay titled, "Which black people should I listen to?" "But what if I settle on a position and then a Black person says I am wrong? That might be uncomfortable, yes. But if your goal is to be a force against racism, not to get the applause of every Black person on earth, it will also be just fine." (*New York Times*: Opinion Section, June 30, 2021)

As our MFE board was considering the Songs For Justice project, we talked a lot about risk. Specifically, what were the risks to the organization and our programming if SFJ went off in an unintended or unexpected direction? What would be the fallout from mistakes we might make? While the project was well intended, would it be worth those risks?

Here's an example. We released the first Songs For Justice record in April 2021. At the time, we had begun work on identifying sponsors, artists, and piano placement locations for our 2021 Keys for the City program. As mentioned earlier, we confronted the question of whether we should put out a Songs For Justice piano. The discussion quickly turned to whether this piano, given what it stood for, might be a target for vandalism from folks who might not necessarily believe in social justice. It could be a way, as twisted and misguided as it is, for someone to make a statement. We also discussed where the piano should be located. There were two options. One was in front of a heavily trafficked well-lit building equipped with several security cameras. While that would certainly have been the safest place to put it, we considered another spot.

The Pennsylvania College of Art and Design's (PCAD) Art Park is nestled between PCAD and the police station. While a relatively small parcel of land, perhaps fifty yards by thirty yards, the park is highly symbolic as it was the ground zero gathering place for the street protests in Lancaster during the civil unrest in Summer 2020. It was sacred ground, but poorly lighted and not secured. The risk of vandalism was real.

As we talked through the issue, we determined that we had no choice but to place the Songs For Justice piano on that sacred plot of land. Like that old poker adage, "In for a nickel, in for a dime," we had to be all in, despite the risk.

But let's talk about real risk.

The risk of getting called out as an individual or the chance our piano might be vandalized pales in comparison to thousands of real, consequential risks that Black folk have taken for over 400 years in the fight to simply be considered equal in their own country.

How about John Lewis and the hundreds of people who marched over the Edmund Pettis Bridge in Selma, Alabama on Bloody Sunday, March 7, 1965? What about the risk they took cresting the bridge to see a bevy of policemen armed and ready to stop the march by any means necessary? Talk about risk! Those marchers were taking the ultimate risk. Each had to know that crossing that bridge put their lives at stake.

John Lewis's experience on the Edmund Pettis bridge is well known, as are the stories of other civil rights icons such as Martin

Luther King, Jr., Medgar Evers, James Cheney, Andrew Goodman, and Michael Schwerner who, in their fight for civil rights, knew they risked their lives and, in the end, paid the ultimate price. And there are literally thousands of other less well-known stories of people risking their lives in the pursuit of civil rights.

Consider the ultimate risk assumed by Charles Deslondes. In January 1811, Deslondes organized what is known as the Louisiana Rebellion, where hundreds of enslaved people marched and then attacked several plantations killing White men and destroying property along the way. Within forty-eight hours, the rebellion was quashed and many of the rebels were slaughtered on site. Certainly, those marchers knew the risk in such rebellion. Yet, despite their fears and the risks, they took brave action, rebelled and paid the ultimate price. (Four Hundred Souls p. 173 - 176)

Or how about the risk thousands of Black Americans took for attempting to vote. As Michael Harriott notes in his essay in the book, *Four Hundred Souls: A Community History of African America, 1619-2019*, "Ku Klux Klan members in North Carolina lynched so many Black voters in 1870 that Governor William Woods Holden declared an insurrection and suspended habeas corpus (the right against unlawful detention) imposing martial law in two counties." (Kendhi & Blain 2021, 235 – 236)

And how about the risk that Black Americans face every time they leave their homes or drive their cars? Or, even when in their homes sleeping peacefully in their own beds as was the case in the death of Breanna Taylor, killed in a botched police raid of her apartment.

We Old White Dudes should get over the fear of risk in becoming a force against racism. Compared to the risks that thousands of enslaved Blacks took in fleeing plantations to head north, or the myriad of risks Blacks assumed in living their everyday lives during the Jim Crow era? By comparison, our risks are nothing.

At its core, this is not about risk. It's about truth. Despite our claims of American exceptionalism and our great democracy and how in America, all are equal, the cold, hard truth is that systemic racism lingers. We must come to terms with that truth. We cannot fear it. We cannot be afraid to take a risk, whether large or small, in the name of justice and basic humanity. A different way to look at stepping up and doing something for the cause is less about taking a risk and more about taking advantage of an opportunity to do something to make a difference. To have a positive impact. To move the ball forward.

Perhaps that's not such a risk after all.

# CHAPTER TWENTY-TWO

# TAKING A KNEE

*"Believe in something. Even if it means sacrificing everything."*

—Colin Kaepernick

Sports and music vividly display how, regardless of background, people can work in concert to accomplish impressive things. The sight of athletes or musicians working together toward a common goal, sharing in the sweat, pain, and sacrifice, powerfully illustrates the possibilities of tolerance, diversity, and integration. Seeing Black athletes and musicians perform on equal footing with their fellow White team and bandmates projects the power of replication in so many other occupations and situations. Much of our society's progress, whether in business or everyday life, derives from racial tolerance and acceptance demonstrated through sports and music. When the public sees athletes and musicians working together, it provides a model for others to emulate.

While many things about organized, elite athletics in America are out of perspective, its power and potential to advance civil and human rights issues is not one of them. Sports' fundamental value of fair play and equal opportunity parallels the fundamental values and principles of civil and human rights. The potential to highlight and advance these values may be sports' most important and greatest strength.

In short, you can't avoid sports as a platform to highlight civil and human rights issues. As with the Songs For Justice project, the same applies to music.

A long line of Black Americans have criticized the nation for its shortcomings, including Martin Luther King Jr., Muhammad Ali,

Frederick Douglass, James Baldwin, Nina Simone, and Colin Kaepernick. Michael Eric Dyson in *Tears We Cannot Stop*, writes, "What some of you are missing is that Kaepernick is the best kind of American there is: one willing to criticize his country precisely because he loves it so much." He adds from James Baldwin, "I love America more than any other country in the world, and, exactly for this reason, I insist on the right to criticize her perpetually." (Dyson 2017, 2021, 115)

Dyson continues. "My friends, none of these Black figures hated the nation. Instead, they simply wanted the nation to straighten up and fly right." (Dyson, 2017, 114) He also describes the difference between nationalism and patriotism as follows: "Nationalism is the uncritical celebration of one's nation regardless of its moral or political virtue. It's summarized in the saying, 'My country, love it or leave it . . . Nationalism is the belief that no matter what one's country does—whether racist, homophobic, sexist, xenophobic, or the like—it must be supported and accepted entirely.

"Patriotism is a bigger, more uplifting virtue. Patriotism is the belief in the best values of one's country, and the pursuit of the best means to realize those values. If the nation strays, then it must be corrected. The patriot is the person who, spotting the need for change, says so clearly and loudly, without hate or rancor. The nationalist is the person who spurns such correction and would rather take refuge in bigotry than fight it." (Dyson 2017, 116)

That is why the criticism and blackballing of Colin Kaepernick for *taking a knee* to draw attention to civil rights issues, while not surprising, was disappointing, nonetheless. One of the most important, powerful, and fundamental justifications for our society's tremendous investment in sports is precisely because it has the potential to break down barriers and push for social change and civil rights. Using sports as a vehicle to highlight these issues is as much a part of sports as the touchdown, home run, or slam dunk.

The way the NFL, on the one hand, and the NBA, and WNBA, on the other, handled the demonstrations of athletic solidarity with the

Black Lives Matter movement illustrates a major difference between football and basketball. While basketball, like jazz, is largely about improvisation and creating as play moves on, football is more about strict choreography and staying on script. Yes, there is a certain amount of structure in basketball, but the inherent nature of the game requires a free-thinking approach that encourages improvisation. A byproduct is that in basketball, the players (often with multi-year contracts) have more control over what transpires on the court during the game, which in turn, translates into a more equal power sharing arrangement between the players and owners off the court. As a result, by virtue of their cultures, the NBA and WNBA granted more flexibility and support to players in their protest activities.

Football's restrictive culture leaves less room for improvisation and free-thinking. Consequently, it was no surprise that the NFL's posture regarding players who supported justice and equity was more reactionary and disciplinary. Much of that reaction is explained by the fact that almost all the NFL owners are White, and the majority of its coaches and front office personnel are White, not to mention that most NFL player contracts are one-year deals with minimal guarantees.

Here's the point.

It rings hollow to justify a tremendous investment in sports as an educational and character-building activity and laud its power to advance a cause that you believe in while at the same time claim sports should be value free when the advocated cause is one you may not believe in.

You can't have it both ways. A civil right is a civil right, whether you want to acknowledge it or not. Rather than vilifying athletes who take a knee or musicians who write protest songs, better we acknowledge and, indeed, celebrate the courage and commitment it takes for them to put their careers and livelihoods on the line for a just cause.

# CHAPTER TWENTY-THREE

## THE "BLACK PROBLEM"

*The way to right wrongs is to shine the light of truth upon them. "*
—Ida B. Wells-Barnett

I s systemic racism in our nation only a "Black problem?"

Some believe so. Politicians, social scientists, and pundits often couch the challenges racism presents in terms of "What is America going to do about its 'Black problem?'" Before going further, we need a time out. Full stop!

Racism is *not* a Black problem. It is an American problem! Framing it otherwise is cynical and misguided, missing the most important point of the analysis. The problem is with the system itself. Yes, it is a problem for Blacks as they must navigate that system. But it hasn't been Black Americans who have created *the problem*. The problem is the system, created, fought for, and maintained by White males. It is akin to blaming the pollution of a river on a particular chemical released into its waters. Yes, the chemical may be *a* problem in that it's carcinogenic, but it's not *the* problem. The problem is lax environmental laws and regulations and uncaring polluters who dump chemicals into our waterways. The chemical is the mean, but laxity of laws is the cause of the problem.

Further, casting racism in America in such terms dehumanizes Black folk. It allows people to completely dismiss the unique humaneness of people of color. As my mother never failed to emphasize, human beings—all human beings—need to be affirmed. Looking at racism as a Black problem allows us to look the other way or cover our eyes and assume no responsibility to change the status quo. It allows Whites to justify their indifference by convincing themselves that it is not their (White people's) problem but rather their (Black people's) problem and thus to believe they have no responsibility to address the problem.

That's the real problem.

# CHAPTER TWENTY-FOUR

## PRESERVING "OUR" HERITAGE

*"Preservation of one's own culture does not require contempt or disrespect for other cultures."*

—Cesar Chavez

ornel West is one of America's most influential and provocative philosophers, political activists, social critics, and intellectuals. The grandson of a Baptist minister, West focuses on the role of race, gender, and class in American society. I learned of him in 1993 when I read his classic treatise on race in America, *Race Matters*. Whether he holds forth through published material or television appearances, I pay attention. I recently came across a ten-part lecture series of his sponsored by Dartmouth College titled, "The Historical Philosophy of W.E.B. DuBois." It was extraordinary.

I've sat in lecture halls and classrooms listening to professors, educators, and intellectuals, far too many to count or name, over many years. This video lecture series was hands down the most informative, challenging, thought provoking, and entertaining lecture series I've ever attended or witnessed.

Among other issues, West explored individual and group heritage and, specifically, how people, especially those of Southern heritage, often defend or celebrate the Confederacy and the legacy of the Civil War. This dynamic has currency as many communities are struggling with how to handle Confederate monuments.

He pointed out that most of these monuments were not erected immediately after the Civil War to commemorate fallen soldiers.

Rather, they were built in the early 1900s, during the Jim Crow era, as symbols of White supremacy. The proliferation of these structures grew from attempts of the United Daughters of the Confederacy (UDC) to rewrite Civil War history. The UDC used the symbolic power of the statues to immortalize Confederacy principles for future generations. The UDC, it should be noted, also sang the praises of the Ku Klux Klan, and denied (the unassailable fact) that the central purpose of the Civil War was to maintain slavery.

Obviously, these statues carry a different meaning for Black Americans.

As with any debate about racism in our nation's history, emotions, and sentiments about these monuments on both sides of the divide, are intense. At one end of the spectrum, these monuments represent and promote White supremacy and have no place in public discourse and should be summarily removed from public spaces. At the other end, preserving the monuments preserves history—the good as well as the bad—so as not to repeat it.

It comes down to which symbols and narratives we want to identify with and celebrate as part of our heritage. West's treatment of this issue was particularly enlightening and, in his inimitable fashion, provocative. At risk of misrepresenting West's ideas, following is a summary of what I gained from his lecture on this issue.

West acknowledges that everyone has a right to preserve their heritage. But he adds that you must be clear about what part of your heritage you claim pride in and are willing to fight to preserve. What part of your heritage are you aligned with? In the case of Southern heritage, it includes believing in some of humanity enslaved in perpetuity. He asks, "Is that the heritage you want to claim? Is that your vision and your argument? Is that really what you are saying?"

He offers Germany as an example. Beethoven and Hitler are both part of German heritage. One induces exaltation, the other revulsion. Similarly, there are wonderful aspects of Southern heritage worth embracing and celebrating. But slavery and Jim Crow? It is a matter of parsing aspects of heritage that are honorable and shameful. West challenges us to be transparent about what aspects of our heritage we want to align ourselves with.

It begins with an honest assessment of the legacies—the good, bad and the ugly—of our heritage. Which to embrace and which to reject. Ultimately, we must determine that for ourselves, aided by hindsight, which often shines a bright light on the past and its impact on our nation's values, institutions, and citizens.

Which parts of your heritage will you decide to embrace and defend . . . or reject?

# CHAPTER TWENTY-FIVE

# THOSE "VIOLENT" BLM PROTESTS

*"This (BLM) isn't a political statement. This is a human rights statement, a fairness statement."*

—Mike Krzyzewski

To say that 2020 and 2021 had its share of civil unrest would be an understatement. From Black Lives Matter protests throughout our nation in the aftermath of the George Floyd's murder, which despite rhetoric from the likes of Fox News were overwhelmingly peaceful, to the violent insurrectionist storming the US Capital on January 6, 2021, it has been a contentious period in our nation's history.

Given how divided we are, it is no surprise that these events have been thoroughly politicized. But it is the narrative around the BLM protests that I find particularly disturbing. The conservative media, pundits, and politicians continue to express their outrage at the purported mass violence that BLM supporters fomented during these protests. By their accounts, the protests and destructive behaviors were extremely widespread and, in their minds, unjustified. This, even though according to a study by the Armed Conflict Location and Event Data Project, only six percent of Black Lives Matter demonstrations last year involved violence—by demonstrators, counterdemonstrators, or police officers—or property destruction. (*New York Times Magazine,* October 31, 2021, 29)

While the protests were widespread and certainly intense, the assertion they were excessively violent is simply not true. A more interesting question is whether they were justified at all. While I do not condone violence, an argument can be made that, given our long and dark history of racism and police brutality against POC, the protests were justified. Frankly, it is surprising that Black Americans have not gone to the streets to protest more often. The 1960s produced widespread protests and violence, and there have been periodic, less extensive protests throughout the years. But given our nation's historical treatment of Blacks as second-class citizens, it's remarkable that Blacks don't take to the streets every day!

Think about it. How would we as Old White Dudes react if the shoe was on the other foot? From slavery to Jim Crow laws, to lynching, to mass incarceration, to police brutality, to structural policy inequities and discrimination in housing, health care and education, to name a sampling, it's a wonder our nation isn't perpetually aflame with violence and protest. Fortunately, we have the teachings of non-violent protest of MLK, John Lewis, Nelson Mandela, and others to thank for that.

Granted, there have been incidences of violence unleashed by Black Americans over issues of racism throughout our history, most notably the unrest that was a part of the civil rights movement in the 1960s. But let's be honest. If we Old White Dudes were continually treated with hatred and second-class citizenship for 24/7/365/400+, wouldn't we lash out? If you kick a man when he is down and continue to kick him relentlessly to keep him down, eventually he will kick back.

But isn't it counterproductive to protest and riot? Why not simply come together to talk about these things? Perhaps. But here's the dirty little secret about instigating racial violence. Whites have done their share of instigating violence on a mass scale against Black communities. In 1921, White residents of Tulsa massacred hundreds of Black citizens and burned down the Greenwood section of town. The significance of that massacre was that at the time Greenwood was one of the wealthiest and most prosperous communities in America. It was known as the Black Wall Street. Apparently, the Whites of Tulsa could not stand for Blacks within *their* community achieving such success. They had to burn it down, literally. There's also the example of the Chicago race riot of 1919, started by Whites, that began on the South Side on July 27 and ended on August 3, during which thirty-eight people died.

These are only two examples. There are many more. William A. Darity, professor of economics and the Samuel DuBois Cook distinguished professor of public policy at Duke University, writing in the *New York Times* (September 24, 2021, Business Section, page 4) about the racial wealth divide, noted that there were "more than 100 well-documented white terrorist massacres from the end of the Civil War through World War II."

He added, "In 1919, known as the 'Red Summer,' about 35 massacres occurred in locales as varied as Bisbee, Ariz.; Chicago; Wilmington, Del.; Elaine, Ark; Washington; and Ocoee, Fla. Black lives were lost to white mob violence, and white terrorists seized and appropriated—stole— Black property. All this deepened the racial wealth divide."

And how many Black churches have been burned to the ground over the years? Scores.

My point is that we, as OWDs, have no business talking about Blacks initiating civil unrest or violent protests. The fact is our lily-white hands are not free of bloodstains.

What is amazing is not that BLM protests broke out after George Floyd's murder, but rather the degree of restraint, non-violence, patience, and love Black Americans exhibited during them. My guess is that if the shoe was on the other foot, things would have escalated to all-out war and anarchy. Simply consider the insurrection at the US Capital on January 6, 2021. It was almost exclusively a White crowd of rioters taking to the streets, attacking police over a completely debunked claim of a stolen election. Rather than accusing Blacks of instigating violence over issues of race and social justice, we'd be well-served to take a long, hard look in the mirror. History doesn't lie. We've not only done the same, but we've done far more of it. Rather than condemning the violence we should be recognizing the patience of Black Americans and their love of country, despite the many reasons they have not to.

While the right-wing media paint a far different picture for purposes of stoking fear, anger, resentment, division, not to mention sponsorship revenue and ratings, I'd encourage you to consider the civil unrest of the summer of 2020 from a historical context. After thoughtfully considering the history, you may come to a different conclusion. There is absolutely nothing wrong with reconsidering your beliefs and changing your mind on an issue, whatever that issue may be. The ability to learn, grow, and be open to rethinking your beliefs or world view is not weakness. It is strength. You do not automatically have to adopt the attitudes, beliefs, and world view of your parents, friends, or favorite television personalities. Reconsidering a particular position or belief when faced with new or different information is a sign of intelligence, confidence, and courage.

Now that you have been provided a bit more context and history around the issue of racial justice protests, perhaps you might reconsider your position on those "exceedingly violent" BLM protests.

# CHAPTER TWENTY-SIX

## CRITICAL RACE THEORY

*"The white man's happiness cannot be purchased with the Black man's misery."*

—Frederick Douglass

Another battle in the fight against racism being fought is how schools teach the history of slavery and racism. Given that these issues remain particularly contentious, coupled with our increasingly polarized society, it is no surprise that the issue has been highly politicized. At the center is the concept of Critical Race Theory (CRT).

Before moving forward, let's be clear about one thing. Critical Race Theory is not being taught in our grade schools and high schools. Claims to the contrary are false. It is, however, taught in law schools. CRT, as an academic concept, posits that racism is a social construct and not merely the product of individual bias or prejudice, but is embedded in legal systems and public policies. Given the crux of the theory, it makes perfect sense to teach the subject in our law schools.

Claiming that CRT is taught in our grade schools and high schools is utterly disingenuous and false. Worse, it is pretexted to discourage or outright ban the teaching of our nation's history relating to racism. The result has been numerous state legislatures proposing and passing bills to ban its teaching in the classroom. The idea that we cannot even acknowledge our sordid history of racism, slavery, and Jim Crow as part of American history because it might make White folks uncomfortable is perhaps the most blatant example of White fragility.

I fully understand that people of all faiths and political persuasion are entitled to their opinions and beliefs. But working to deny the ability to teach US history with little mention of the role that slavery and racism has played is irresponsible and dangerous. It shows how White fragility can cause us to avoid recognition of our responsibilities as White people not simply to work towards eliminating racism and injustice in our society, but for even making the effort to understand the root and causes of those injustices.

How can we teach basic, fundamental US history without referencing slavery, Jim Crow, and the civil rights movement? We cannot. The institution of slavery is often referred to as America's original sin. It is a fundamental, bedrock piece of our collective history. You can't ignore it. It happened. This is another example of Whites having to deal with the world as it is rather than how we want to believe it is—or was.

This begs the question. What are we afraid of? If, as we like to say, "I didn't enslave or lynch anyone and don't actively perpetuate racism," why would we cover our ears and close our eyes to that history?

These events, issues, and policies all happened. They are historical facts. They are a part of our collective national story. It's time we faced that head on. You can't sweep our common history under the rug as those who ignore history are bound to repeat it. The fact is that Blacks, and Whites have been, are currently, and forever will be, bound together as Americans. Our history is a shared history, warts and all. If there has ever been an example of the possibility of "the truth setting us free," this might be it.

# CHAPTER TWENTY-SEVEN

# INDIVIDUAL BEHAVIOR VS. PERCEPTIONS OF GROUPS

*"The cost of liberty is less than the price of repression."*
—W.E.B. DuBois

**W**hen it comes to issues of race, there is a difference between individual and group behavior. The difference slices both ways. For example, if I do something criminal, it does not mean that everyone in any particular group I am associated with or a part of are also criminals. Conversely, the general behavior or beliefs of a group or organization does not necessarily reflect the behavior or beliefs of every individual in that group. Yet, it seems that when it comes to race, many people tend to think in those terms.

Ibram X. Kendi offers definitions of this mindset in his book, *How to be an Anti-Racist*.

"*Behavioral Racist*: One who is making individuals responsible for the perceived behavior of racial groups and making racial groups responsible for the behavior of individuals.

*Behavioral Antiracist*: One who is making racial group behavior fictional and individual behavior real." (Kendhi 2019, 92)

I found his perspective and explanation around the issue of behavior particularly interesting. Kendi freely admits that he was not the most engaged student as a teenager. Regardless, he used his lackluster academic performance in high school to make his point.

"How do we think about my young self, the C or D student, in antiracist terms. The truth is that I should be critiqued as a student; I was undermotivated and distracted and undisciplined. In other words,

a bad student. But I shouldn't be critiqued as a bad *Black* student.
I did not represent my race any more than my irresponsible White
classmates represented their race. It makes racist sense to talk about
personal irresponsibility as it applies to an entire racial group. Racial-
group behavior is a figment of the racist's imagination. Individual
behaviors can shape the success of individuals. But policies determine
the success of groups. And it is racist power that creates the policies
that cause racial inequities.

"Making individuals responsible for the perceived behavior of racial
groups and making whole racial groups responsible for the behavior
of individuals are the two ways that behavioral racism infects our
perception of the world. In other words, when we believe that a racial
group's seeming success or failure redounds to each of its individual
members, we've accepted a racist idea. Likewise, when we believe that
an individual's seeming success or failure redounds to an entire group,
we've accepted a racists idea." (Kendhi 2019, 94)

Kendi also addresses this issue in his book *Stamped From the
Beginning*, where he writes, "[N]o racial group has ever had a monopoly
on any type of human trait or gene—not now, not ever. Under our
different looking hair and skin doctors cannot tell the difference
between our bodies, our brains, or the blood that runs in our veins. All
cultures, in all their behavioral differences, are on the same level. Black
Americans history of oppression has made Black opportunities—not
Black people—inferior." (Kendhi 2016, 11)

In short, there are often behaviors or beliefs that are associated
with a particular group. But that does not mean that every individual
believes in or exhibits behaviors that always reflect those group
behaviors and beliefs. It's a simple notion but one that we often forget
when considering issues around racism.

It is not enough to claim not to be racist. Rather, you should
actively denounce or oppose various racist notions, regardless of how
widely believed. This runs parallel to the idea that silence is no longer
an option. Racist ideas and beliefs must be actively challenged and

called out—repeatedly—including the differences between group and individual behavior.

# CHAPTER TWENTY-EIGHT

# RACISM AND DEMOCRACY

*"Where you see wrong or inequality or injustice, speak out. This is your democracy. Make it. Protect it. Pass it on."*

—Thurgood Marshall

When it comes to American democracy and the principle that we are all created equal, we Old White Dudes have some explaining to do. First, we should acknowledge that from the beginning we didn't have a genuine democracy for the simple reason that not everyone was treated equally. And we should acknowledge that OWDs established, fought for, and continue to resist changes to the status quo.

How else can you explain why the modern-day Republican Party, overwhelmingly White and male, is so enraptured with Donald Trump? There is no shortage of evidence that Trump is a racist. He stoked racial division not simply during his presidential campaign, but for years beforehand, and he continues today. Trump's not-so-subtle message is that White Americans need to take back and maintain absolute control of all levels of government, industry, and media. Clearly, many Trumpers believe the United States of America is "their" (White) country and theirs alone.

It's not.

Black Americans have fought and died for this country and its supposed "freedom and equal opportunity." They did all that, despite, for example, fighting in World War II to defeat fascism and Nazism, only to find, upon returning home, that the rights for which they fought overseas were not granted them at home.

The current assault on democracy is being played out around issues relating to voting rights and voter suppression. Organized efforts to purge Black voters from the voting rolls or eliminate Sunday "Souls to the Polls" are rising. How is that any different than requiring Black voters to pay a poll tax or guess the exact number of jellybeans in a jar to vote, as occurred during Jim Crow? Different methods and techniques, but the same purpose, excluding POC from using the constitutional right to vote to achieve equal rights. How can this be justified?

In short, there is an alarming number of people who believe the US is a White nation and want their White legacy celebrated and preserved at the expense of Black Americans—at any cost. Like it or not, we are a diverse nation, a nation of immigrants, and becoming more so. Nothing will change those trends. Get used to it.

# CHAPTER TWENTY-NINE

## ON RAP AND HIP HOP

*"We can't change the world unless we change ourselves."*

—Biggie Smalls (The Notorious B.I.G)

For the past ten years, MFE has been conducting a monthly concert series every third Friday from May through September where we book up to thirty different acts throughout downtown. During that time, we have sponsored literally hundreds of Music Friday acts.

Unfortunately, we have been negligent in not offering rap and hip-hop as a music alternative during Music Fridays. We are not proud of that. Delving into the SFJ project provided a harsh reminder of how we had fallen in our quest to become a diverse organization. It is also an example of something we have sought to rectify. One of the direct benefits of undertaking the Songs For Justice project has been how it introduced us to a diverse range of musicians and musical acts. It's allowed us to begin booking a more diverse palette of musicians, including rap and hip-hop artists for various events. As a result, we have experienced some interesting moments.

Here's an example.

From the beginning, we have had only one negative interaction with the local police during Music Fridays. It occurred because a band was playing too loud. Given that history, it was interesting what occurred during the first rap and hip-hop show we booked for Music Friday. The audience was not particularly large (perhaps fifty to seventy-five people), the crowd was mostly people of color, including some children, and all the performers were POC. Twenty minutes into the show, a White police officer showed up and, for no apparent reason, began to ask questions. He complained he had not been told about the event, even though we partner with the city on these events. He said while he wasn't intending to "shut the show down," the performers had better "watch their language" or they'd each run the risk of getting hit with fines.

Coincidence? Really? Sadly, my guess is that this officer was trying to flex his White privilege power. He saw a bunch of Black folk having too much fun—or experiencing too much freedom—and couldn't resist putting these folks *in their place*.

I was not there at the time and the Black musicians running the stage handled it. I'm guessing they've been there before. It got me to thinking about how I would have handled that situation.

Full disclosure. I've not listened to much rap and hip-hop, although I am getting exposure through the SFJ project. I much prefer jazz and blues, although they share some musical elements. And yes, rap and hip-hop can be direct, in your face, and sometimes angry. But so can other music. This time, I was somewhat familiar with the material because of the musicians' involvement with Songs For Justice. While some was challenging and direct, the vast majority was positive, addressing topics like personal responsibility, believing in yourself, coming together as a community, and doing good in this world.

I have never encountered a situation where the police felt the need to intervene because of the color of my skin. Even if it happened, I doubt I'd have to worry about an escalating situation or sense that my life was in danger. That is not the case for Black folk. When I asked the stage manager about the incident, he rolled his eyes, shook his head, and said, "Welcome to our world."

So, with the advantage of hindsight, this is what I would have said. "Sir, can you stay and visit for a few minutes? Let's listen to what these performers are saying."

This is what he would have heard. The first set of lyrics was written by Terian Mack. Titled "Believe," the song was featured on Side A of Songs For Justice Volume One:

*Believe believe believe*
*321 hey*

*Chorus*

*I believe in me I believe in you I believe in we now think about*
*what we could do*
*what we could do*
*If we just get together*
*we getting together no matter the weather*
*we getting together feeling to get there*
*now say it together yeah*

*I believe in me I believe in you I believe in we now think about*
*what we could do*
*What we could do*
*If we just get together*
*We getting together no matter the weather*
*We getting together feeling together*
*Now say it together yea*

*Verse 1*

*I believe in me I believe in you I believe in we now think about*
*what you can do*
*What you can do*
*If you just get up and apply yourself*
*to supply your wealth*
*because right around the corner*
*your dreams may lie*
*you'll never know if you don't go outside*
*you better get up and go chase it*
*keep your passion and pride in your pocket don't you lose it and*

*don't get lost*
*in the illusion or stuck in the matrix*
*it's time to awaken*
*because times never waiting*
*yeah no waiting no waiting no waiting*
*still Blazin still Blazin still Blazin*
*time to get up and make all those changes*
*I hope you believe when I say this yea*

*Chorus*

*I believe in me I believe in you I believe in we now think about*
*what we could do*
*what we could do*
*If we just get together*
*we getting together no matter the weather*
*we getting together feeling to get there*
*now say it together yeah*
*No waiting no waiting no waiting*
*Still Blazin still Blazin still Blazin*
*Time to wake up and make all them changes I hope you believe*
*when I say this yea*

*Verse 2*

*I believe in me I believe in you I believe that we now think*
*about what we could do*
*what we could do, if we all unite tonight*
*Better hold in tight*
*Because right around he corner*
*Your fears will hide*
*You better step outside and don't be scared*
*Look up to the sky I know he is there*

*Watching down on you*
*Reigning down*
*All powerful*
*Now that you got it*
*this was made to pump you up*
*Something you can listen to*
*Right Before you go to work*
*Something you can play*
*when you sit alone at lunch*
*Something you can play*
*Every day of the month*
*Perform this live and make the world*
*Fall in love*
*My goal is to serenade the masses*
*Even from the casket*
*Can you imagine?*

He would have also heard the following song, titled *Right Now*, performed by Sir Dominique Jordan, The Prolific One:

*Right Now*
*I Can . . . I can,*
*I Will . . . I will,*
*but when?*
*Right Now*

*Heart of a starving Lion,*
*Despite all the deprivation,*
*Elated and highly favored,*
*Still waiting but quite impatient,*
*Sorry for being abrasive,*
*But the hate so real that irks my soul*

*I guarantee this, it won't stop my growth, fear ain't real, I stay oh so bold, what's a set back to a real one whom equipped to prevent that... used to be a used to til I realized it's all about the get back . . . (say that)*

*I Can, I can*
*I Will, I will*
*But when? But when?*
*Right now!*

*Remain Tru2You, master your skills and elevate, if you nervous to practice, how you gonna win, no time to pretend, you gotta activate the real you from inside that's hiding from the planet, when you find it, you'll do some damage to anything tryna slander your destiny which is written in the sky, as long as you see what you can be, anything's possible,*
*now be great and fly!*

Watch out, White America! Those are some dangerous ideas these two hip-hop artists are espousing! We might need to shut them down!

Too many White folks look at rappers and hip-hop artists and automatically assume that what they are singing is divisive and hateful. Again, rap and hip-hop can be harsh. But the same thing applies to many other types of music, including Goth and Heavy Metal. We should not assume that if the musician or performer is Black or if he or she is performing a particular style of music that the music is hateful or divisive. There is a wide variety of music out there, many styles, many sounds, and many messages. Don't dismiss any of it based simply upon the color of the skin of the performer or the style of music.

If you took some time and listened to what many rap and hip-hop artists are singing about, it might surprise you. In other words, if we want to fight against racism, we must be open to alternative cultural expression and art forms performed by people who do not look like us. Or, in the words of Terian Mack:

> *I believe in me I believe in you I believe in we now think about*
> *what we could do*
> *what we could do*
> *If we just get together*

# CHAPTER THIRTY

## REPLACEMENT THEORY

*"My father was a slave and my people died to build this country and I am going to stay here and have a part of it just like you."*

—Paul Robeson

A disturbingly prevalent pretext developing among White nationalists is the Replacement Theory, which argues that nonwhite immigrants are being imported (sometimes the Jewish community is tarred with orchestrating this) to "replace" White people and White voters. The purported goal is for non-White culture to replace White culture through mass migration and immigration. In other words, Jews and people of color are taking over the government and society to marginalize Whites. It originally took hold in France and throughout Europe and has gained traction in the US.

This ideology was on full display during the 2007 far-right rally in Charlottesville, Virginia when crowds of White men marched with torches chanting "Jews will not replace us." More recently, it reared its ugly head again at the January 6, 2021, insurrection at the US capital.

Political scientist Robert Pape studied the 380 or so people arrested in connection with that insurrection. According to the *New York Times*, Pape "expected to find that the rioters were driven to violence by the lingering effects of the 2008 Great Recession. Instead, he found something different. His polling and demographic data showed that most of the insurrectionists were motivated by the fear that the rights of minorities and immigrants were crowding out the rights of white people in American politics and culture." (*New York Times*, April 7, 2021, p. A-15)

The spread of such a hateful, racist ideology is frightening. Federal authorities now indicate that American extremists are the most urgent terrorist threat to the country. Since January 6, 2021, researchers have identified members of more than a dozen extremist groups that took part in the Trump-fueled riot. The storming of the Capital drew extremists that included QAnon conspiracists, the far-right group the Proud Boys, militiamen, White supremacists, and die-hard Trump supporters. And who makes up most of these groups? White men.

Yes, the demographics of our country are changing. We are becoming more diverse and less White. But that is the result of broad demographic changes and not a sinister plot to eliminate or replace White culture. America is a nation of immigrants. Always has been. And it is the vibrant mix of people of all nationalities, backgrounds, and colors, that is our greatest strength. The fact is racists' revisionist theory is simply a harmful, hateful, divisive lie.

Want to know something that you can do to be a positive force for social and racial justice? The next time you hear someone spout this Replacement Theory nonsense, call them on it!

# CHAPTER THIRTY-ONE

# PEONAGE

*"To deny people their human rights is to challenge their very humanity"*
—Nelson Mandela

When you are interested in learning about a topic, you sometimes notice things that escaped you previously. Maybe it's a random newspaper column, or hearing someone on television refer to an obscure fact about the topic. It's like having a special antenna that detects nuances about the subject and sends an alert to your brain to *pay attention. Check this out.* These brain signals often are triggered in the most unlikely places, including Facebook.

I try to spend as little time on Facebook as possible, but I do periodically check on some posts. During a recent Facebook visit, a black and white image of about thirty Black prisoners working in a field popped up on the feed. The title was "Here is the Truth Behind Systemic Racism." Generally, my approach to Facebook is "don't trust, always verify." After fact checking and confirming the historical accuracy of the information, it became another example of how little I, and most others, know about the history of systemic racism in our country.

The issue is *peonage.*

Peonage, also called debt slavery or debt servitude, is a system where an employer compels a worker to pay off a debt with work.

I suspect that, like me, most OWDs have a shallow understanding of the peonage and sharecropping systems. And much like me, most OWDs have no understanding of how sordid a system it was. Here's a brief explanation.

Peonage was a form debt servitude whereby Blacks were accused of falsely owing money or trivial sums, given sham trials, and deemed by the courts to be beholden to one-way contracts to provide labor to work down debt. The peonage contracts often allowed the creditor to trade, confine, whip and beat workers if there was an outstanding debt, which for many could be forever.

Congress outlawed peonage in 1867, and not missing a beat, White landowners replaced it effectively with sharecropping, an analogous system. Sharecropping was an arrangement where a farmer (cropper) would rent land, supplies, including seeds and tools, working animals, and housing from a landowner. In exchange, the cropper would pay the landowner/employer a share of the sold crop to pay off the debt. If the cropper earned more money than the amount of debt, he would keep that money. If, however, the cropper was unable to pay the full debt, that debt carried over to the next season.

Like peonage, the system was ripe for exploitation as the landowner would often take advantage of the cropper by cooking the books or charging outlandish fees. In short, the system was rigged to keep workers in debt and servitude to the landowner.

But the history of peonage and sharecropping in the South is darker. While landowners did not outright own debt servants and sharecroppers, as a practical matter, both were privatized forms of debt slavery. Seems straightforward enough.

But here's where it gets sordid.

While the thirteenth amendment was passed in 1865 and with it the abolishment of slavery and involuntary servitude, an exception got written into the law. Specifically, involuntary servitude (peonage) was outlawed "except as a punishment for a crime." And true to form, White businessmen, landowners, judges, and politicians exploited that exception to create laws and a system that, while not outright slavery, was pretty close to it. It was the need for cheap labor in the form of mostly Black Americans that drove the system. And like the current methods to disenfranchise Blacks through the criminal justice and incarceration system, OWDs began to establish laws to criminalize Blacks to place them in the criminal justice system because their debt and involuntary servitude would be legal as punishment for a crime. Thus, Black men were picked up for minor or severely trumped-up charges, such as vagrancy, if they could not prove they had a job. When they could not pay the fines associated with those charges, they were imprisoned.

Meanwhile, the prison system, recognizing a chance to make money off the backs of free Black labor, would lease the prisoners to local farmers or industrialists, providing cheap labor for their businesses. Often, the payment and debt records were poorly kept or lost, thus compounding the impact. Many Blacks were trapped in an inescapable situation. The system of peonage was not completely eradicated until the 1940s.

Was it outright slavery? Perhaps not. But it was darn close to it. Its enslavement of another sort.

How many of us OWDs ever heard about or were taught this in our schools? It's another example of how systemic racism has been whitewashed from our history.

# CHAPTER THIRTY-TWO

# THE MAGICAL NEGRO

*"Real magic in relationships means an absence of judgment of others."*

—Wayne Dyer

One of the pleasant surprises encountered during my journey has been learning about various unexpected racial and equity issues at the most unexpected times and unexpected ways. In this case, it was my education regarding the *Magical Negro*. I had no idea that such a term or concept was even a thing until Tony Collins, who contributed an essay for the "Voices to be Heard" chapter of this book, schooled me. We were talking about representation of POC on various boards of directors, civic groups, government agencies or task forces. I had remarked that it seemed to me that, at least in our city of Lancaster, the same few POC were always tapped to serve on them. He responded that it was a product of the Magical Negro (or, as Tony called it the Nannygate or Butlerville) trope or cliché.

I hadn't considered that there is a history of many White people, organizations, companies, and industries that, in their efforts to be more inclusive and diverse, are careful only to provide those opportunities to POC who are not too controversial or outspoken. He noted that far too many POC considered and selected by the White establishment are looked at as being safe, and who won't rock the boat too much. He offered the film industry in Hollywood to illustrate his point, using Sidney Poitier's character in the 1967 film *Guess Who's Coming to Dinner?* as an example. The film tells the story of a White woman bringing her Black boyfriend to her home to meet her White parents for dinner. Tony suggested that for the White audience to accept a Black man in such a role, he had to possess impeccable characteristics and credentials. In this case, Poitier's character was impeccably well-dressed and exceedingly well mannered, well spoken, very smart and, as a doctor, extremely accomplished. Casting him in this way was necessary to make the White parents (and audience) comfortable with a Black man coming into their home. Rather than the White parents having to work to make their guest comfortable, which should always be standard operating procedure, in this case, the onus was on the Black man to make his White hosts comfortable. In other words, he had to jump through hoops to make his Blackness *safe* before White folks considered him *acceptable*.

As it turns out, there is a long history of such typecasting in Hollywood.

According to Wikipedia, "In the cinema of the United States, the Magical Negro is a supporting stock character who comes to the aid of white protagonists. Magical Negro characters, who often possess special insight or mystical powers, have long been a tradition in American fiction. A trope, the term was popularized in 2001 by film director Spike Lee while discussing films with students during a tour of college campuses, in which he said Hollywood continued to employ this premise, expressing dismay. He also said that the *The Green Mile* and *The Legend of Bagger Vance* used the *super-duper Magical Negro*. Critics use the word Negro because it is considered archaic, and usually offensive, in modern English. This underlines their message that a magical Black character who goes around selflessly helping White people is a throwback to stereotypes such as the *Sambo* or *noble savage*."

What does this all mean and how does it apply to the subject matter and purpose of this book?

My purpose in bringing up the issue of the Magical Negro is not to critique Hollywood. While the primary thrust of this book is to explore the issue of race, civil rights, and equity, underlying that general thrust is to highlight how issues of diversity impact our lives, businesses, organizations, and communities. It is about how to leverage diversity as a benefit to add value to our lives, businesses, and civic institutions. In other words, it is about making progress, whether personal, organizational, as a business, or community. To achieve any real measure of progress on these issues requires making room at the table for the viewpoints and perspectives of POC. But simply making room for those voices is not enough if the POC asked to join the table are always the same, safe POC.

It is no stretch to say that many White *gatekeepers*, those with the power to identify and invite POC to the table, seem to have a tendency only to invite POC who make the White power structure feel safe. This is like an organization feeling good about itself by publishing a social justice statement, slapping a BLM sign on their front window, and moving on to other issues. That's not enough. Simply inviting a POC onto a board or civic organization is insufficient if the types of POC who are invited are the same, safe candidates who are unable or unwilling to rock the boat in any meaningful way. If we expect to make progress, we've got to make room at the table for POC who might not be Magical Negroes, but rather individuals who are disruptors not afraid to rock the boat by raising difficult issues and generating uncomfortable conversations. That means we must look beyond the usual POC candidates for such positions to include a wider range, whether by age, occupation, socio-economic status, talents, perspectives, and life experiences.

At the end of the day, this is about those who control the existing power structure ceding power. As mentioned, ceding power is difficult. But if we are truly committed as individuals, businesses, or civic organizations to meaningfully address these issues, we cannot let our White fragility get in the way. The fact is the days when you can give these issues and the debate around them cursory attention and consideration are fading rapidly. The push for a more diverse society and power structure, and all the work that is necessary to achieve those goals, will not diminish. These issues can no longer be avoided or pushed under the rug simply because addressing them makes us White folk uncomfortable. They've got to be dealt with.

But what Tony also pointed out, which was eye opening for me, was that as uncomfortable as it might be for White folks to navigate having a POC on a board, commission, or task force, it pales in comparison to the angst and challenges of POC around whether and how much to speak truth to power in those settings. If you remain silent, you might have a hard time looking yourself in the mirror the next morning. But if you speak up, you risk being labeled an angry Black person and you will likely not be asked to be a part of such committees, boards, etc. in the future. As a result, you remove yourself from being at the table and your opportunity to make a difference moving forward. That's a challenging and gut-wrenching balance to strike. While it may seem to be empowering to be in the role of Magical Negro, it comes at a price. Once again, it goes back to the issue of just how exhausting being a POC in America must be. That is something that we, as OWD's, must be cognizant of and sensitive to. As leaders of these organizations, it is inherent upon us to not be satisfied with simply seating a POC at the table. We must encourage and challenge POC to speak up, speak out and tell of their realities. After all, isn't that why they were invited to the table in the first place? To hear and consider their perspective? If not, why go through the charade of inviting them?

Which begs another question. If the pressure to address these issues honestly and directly is only going to increase, rather than looking at these challenges as burdens, why not consider them opportunities? As an individual, business, or civic organization, why not flip the script and look at them as a chance to improve and become stronger and more effective? Having a diverse group of perspectives and decision makers around the table leads to better, more thorough, and informed decisions. The more perspectives and viewpoints, from the tame and safe to the controversial and challenging, the better decisions and outcomes.

If we are committed to becoming better and more effective individually and collectively, it's going to require difficult and challenging conversations. As with any difficult or challenging issue, meaningful progress occurs only when we must consider, contemplate, and directly address those issues. In other words, addressing difficult, systemic issues often requires a bit of boat rocking. But that won't happen if the POC who are allowed to be at the table are required to jump through hoops to be perceived as safe and acceptable to the guardians of the status quo. In other words, to be *magical*.

# CHAPTER THIRTY-THREE

## HAVING A "PURE HEART"

*"You should never be fearful about doing what you are doing when it is right."*

—Rosa Parks

When it comes to racism, I've come to realize that simply claiming that my heart is in the right place or that my heart is pure is not as straightforward as it seems. In fact, it can be argued that such an attitude contributes to the perpetuation of racism. Robin DiAngelo opened my eyes to this in her book *Nice Racism: How Progressive White People Perpetuate Racial Harm*. She forced me to rethink my use of that descriptor. She refers to a "culture of niceness."

"How often have you heard a white person respond to a charge of racism against a friend by gathering other friends and colleagues to testify that he or she cannot be racist because 'he or she is a really nice person' or 'volunteers on the board of a non-profit serving underprivileged youth' or 'dated a POC.' Characteristics of a culture of niceness include white solidarity, avoiding, causing, or experiencing social discomfort, focusing on connections and commonalities, privileging concern for the feelings of the perpetrators of racism over the victims, helping others to maintain face, and elevating intentions over impact. Intentions are particularly important in a culture of niceness.

"Niceness requires that racism only be acknowledged in acts that *intentionally* hurt or discriminate, which means that racism can rarely be acknowledged. Being nice also allows for absolution: if they didn't intend to perpetuate racism, the act cannot and should not count." (DiAngelo 2021, 49)

DiAngleo is correct in that claiming that having a pure heart does not give you a free pass to say or do racist things. And it certainly does not give you a free pass on having to do serious self-reflection regarding the impact of your words or actions. As a result, I have come to believe that having a pure heart on these issues means the following:

- You acknowledge that as a white person you have tremendous privilege.
- You've decided you will be a part of the solution.
- You are committed to doing the necessary work to learn how your actions, words, and assumptions contribute to the problem.
- You are committed to critical, honest self-reflection regarding how you have contributed to the problem and are willing learn, grow, and improve.
- You commit to acting to help create an all-inclusive America.

Most people do not want to commit racist acts. But it is difficult to avoid racist behaviors when you have lived in a segregated all-White world your entire life. So, yes, in your heart you do not believe you are racist. But after enjoying and benefitting from a lifetime of White privilege, it's not surprising that some of those beliefs, behaviors, and habits have rubbed off. As Robin DiAngelo says, it is the impact of those actions that do the damage regardless of intentions. Those with the best of intentions and purest of hearts must learn to understand that.

Here is another way to drive this point home, again in the words of Robin DiAngelo: "[S]topping our racist patterns must be more important than working to convince others we don't have them. We do have them, and people of color already know we have them; our efforts to prove otherwise are not convincing. An honest accounting of these patterns is no small task given the power of white fragility and white solidarity, but it is necessary," (DiAngelo 2018, 129).

In short, when it comes to having a pure heart in matters relating to racism and social justice, it's not our intentions that matter, but rather our words and actions. So, what are you going to do, rather than simply claim, to demonstrate that your heart is, in fact, pure?

# CHAPTER THIRTY-FOUR

## EMPATHY, GRACE, AND FORGIVENESS

*"The old law of an eye for an eye, leaves everyone blind."*

—Martin Luther King, Jr.

In today's super charged, divided political environment, we often demonize those who don't agree with us. I recently read an article about Thurgood Marshall that forced me to rethink my inclination to occasionally do the same.

Marshall was a civil rights lawyer and American icon who argued many of the cases that broke down America's color line. He won twenty-nine of the thirty-two cases he argued before the US Supreme Court and eventually became the first Black Supreme Court justice. The article was written by Stephen L. Carter, who served as one of his law clerks. It appeared in the *New York Times Magazine* on July 18, 2021. Carter marveled at how Marshall would often socialize with dyed-in-the-wool segregationists, even mentioning that some were good people. These days, we all might ask, how in the world could he say and do that?

Here is how Carter explained it:

"To the Judge, those who disagreed with him on the most important moral issue of the 20th century in America did not thereby lose their humanity. How is that possible? Because he was able to reach across that deep moral divide and find commonalities with those on the other side. Only rarely did he see his opponents as evil; most were simply misguided. People, he knew, can be complicated." (27)

Michael Dyson writes about the power of empathy and the

importance of "walking a mile in the boots of blackness" in his work, *Tears We Cannot Stop*. Here are, in part, the final two paragraphs of his book:

"The siege of hate will not end until white folk imagine themselves as black folk—vulnerable despite our virtues. If enough of you, one by one, exercises your civic imagination, and puts yourself in the shoes of your black brothers and sisters, you might develop a democratic impatience for injustice, for the cruel disregard of black life, for the careless indifference to our plight."

"Empathy can be cultivated. The practice of empathy means taking a moment to imagine how you might behave if you were in our positions. Do not tell us how we should act if we were you; imagine how you would act if you were us. Imagine living in a society where your white skin marks you for distrust, hate and fear. Imagine that for many moments. Only when you see black folk as we are and imagine yourselves as we have to live our lives, only then will the suffering stop, the hurt cease, the pain go away." (Dyson 2017, 2021, 212)

I offer these passages to reaffirm an important lesson I learned from my parents. Regardless of our backgrounds or opinions, it serves us well to recognize everyone's humanity and, in doing so, we can find common ground regardless of political ideology. Or at a minimum, make an honest attempt to do so.

It leads to another story that is instructive. Writing in the *New York Times*, Nicholas Kristoff tells the story of Darryl Davis, a Black musician who has a rather unusual calling. "He hangs out with Ku Klux Klan members and neo-Nazis and chips away at their racism. He has evidence of great success: a collection of KKK robes given him by people whom he persuaded to abandon the Klan . . . There's something to be said for the basic Davis inclination toward dialogue even with unreasonable antagonists. If we're all stuck in the same boat, we should talk to each other."

Kristoff continues, "At a time when America is so polarized and political space is so toxic, we, of course, have to stand up for what we think is right. But it may also help to sit down with those we believe are wrong." (*New York* Times: Sunday Review, June 27, 2021, 7)

Speaking of talking to each other, it is fair to say that a lot of us OWDs feel under attack when it comes to the discussion of racial justice. While that might be considered as our White fragility creeping to the surface, it is something that can feel very real. Many White people feel cowed and are intimidated into silence. As a result, we don't feel that we can say, question, or challenge anything relating to race and social justice.

But we shouldn't let that paralyze us into silence. We can, in fact, ask questions and even challenge certain assumptions, regardless of who expresses them. But here is the key. In doing so, we must be respectful, humble, empathetic, and most important, open minded and willing to learn and change our beliefs and behaviors. If we have questions or a different opinion on an issue, we shouldn't feel we cannot express those thoughts or impressions. Being able to ask questions and talk about points of contention in a civilized and respectful manner is critical in engaging in the type of productive dialogue that can result in change. It is only when that dialogue is approached with an open mind, a genuine willingness to learn, and a profound sense of humility and respect that true understanding and progress can be achieved. So, yes, you can express your opinions, even when controversial, provided you are open to the possibility you may be challenged and corrected if they are misguided. And when they are misguided, you should recognize it, learn why they are misguided or hurtful, and be willing to change your perspective or opinions accordingly.

So much of the path to reconciliation depends on our ability to understand and empathize with POC and their everyday realities. The more we can engage in those honest, difficult discussions, the greater our capacity and ability to engage in more of them. It's like a muscle that can be built up with repeated use and exercise. The more we train and build up our empathy, grace, and forgiveness muscle, the better we will become at understanding each other and reconciling our differences.

I'll leave the final thought on this subject to Darryl Davis. "If I can sit down and talk to KKK members and neo-Nazis and get them to give me their robes and hoods and swastika and all that crazy kind of stuff," Davis said, "there's no reason why somebody can't sit down at a dinner table and talk to their family member." (*New York Times*: Sunday Review, June 27, 2021, 7)

The empathy, grace, and forgiveness of Black Americans is extraordinary. How can we not recognize, accept, and embrace that? Once again, ask yourself how you would respond and act given such a history if the shoe was on the other foot. Particularly when those shoes have been beaten up, are worn out, without laces, and have big holes in the soles. I wonder whether we would be capable of showing such empathy, grace, and forgiveness.

# CHAPTER THIRTY-FIVE

# LIVING IN A POST-RACIAL SOCIETY?

*"Unfortunately, 'post racism' is also a myth, like unicorns and Black people who survive until the end of the movie."*

—Justin Simien

It's often been said we now live in a post-racial society simply because Barack Obama was elected president, twice. For those who believe that I have a few questions.

Are we in a post-racial society when, at any random moment, you might get shot during a routine traffic stop? Or, in the case of George Floyd, suffocated to death in plain view, or Breanna Taylor, the medical worker shot and killed by Louisville police during a botched raid on her apartment? Is that post-racial? Or, because of a minor drug possession charge you are incarcerated, labeled a felon and not only have to spend time in prison, but upon release, are stripped of many fundamental rights and denied access to jobs and other benefits of being an American citizen at a far greater percentage rate than Whites? Is that post-racial?

Is it reasonable to think that we have achieved a post-racial world when the horrors of the Jim Crow era are not that far behind us and continue to have impact? Yes, in some ways Jim Crow was an improvement over being enslaved. Yet, Black Americans still had to live with the reality that, at any random moment and for the most innocuous reason, they might be lynched by an angry mob of Ku Klux Klan members. Or think of fourteen-year-old Emmitt Till, who on August 28, 1955, while visiting family in Money, Mississippi was brutally murdered for allegedly flirting with a White woman four days earlier, an assertion retracted by the woman years later. That was in 1955. Not too long ago. To think we are in a post racial society because of the passage of a few civil rights laws, with those memories and realities still in plain view in our rearview mirror, is far-fetched.

Having a Black president and woman of color vice president does not mean we now live in a post-racial world. We should acknowledge systematic racism still exists and assume some personal responsibility to do something to change it.

It's time to go on record. Not simply with words, or intent, but with work and action. It's time to look into the mirror and ask yourself, "Where exactly do I stand? And what am I willing to do to contribute to building a more inclusive America?"

The fact is, we've got a lot more work to do.

# CHAPTER THIRTY-SIX

## ON BEING "WOKE"

*"Intellectual growth should commence at birth and cease only at death."*
—Albert Einstein

In Chapter Eleven I explained that chapters twelve through thirty-eight should be considered an issues grab bag. I also explained how my understanding of the various issues addressed was mixed. On some of them I feel well-informed and comfortable in offering an opinion, while on others I am still working my way through all the angles and nuances. I also mentioned that on others, I have far more questions than answers. I am not sure what to think of *wokeness,* the issue explored here.

In no way do I want to sound glib or to undervalue or dismiss the many very intense feelings that this term evokes. I understand how the term gained currency as it has been applied to issues relating to our ongoing public debate about racism, justice, and equity. And that its use has accelerated during the racial unrest of the past few years. My impression from the public debate around the term is that it has come to represent not simply the desire to learn facts about social justice, but that it implies a willingness to actively work on being more aware of and in tune with issues of social justice.

I am having a hard time understanding why this term has sparked such widespread angst and division. Conservatives and the political right use it as a slur, while liberals and the political left consider it a badge of honor.

When in doubt, particularly where language and words and their meanings are involved, you go to the primary source—the dictionary. According to Merriam-Webster, the definition of woke is to be "aware of and actively attentive to important facts and issues (especially issues of racial and social justice)."

What is so disappointing is that the political right who use the term disparagingly want to block attempts to learn accurate history think so poorly of people. Apparently, they do not trust people to be smart and thoughtful enough to be exposed to truth, facts, and history, or able to decide for themselves what to think of that history. Do they believe that people are too fragile or immature to handle the truth? A better approach, it seems to me, would be to expose people to facts and truth and trust that they can make their own decisions. Perhaps on matters like these we would be better served to, once again, trust people's better angels.

My question is simple. What is so bad about being aware of and attentive to facts and issues about any subject, including racial justice? What is wrong with being curious regarding facts and truth? Isn't that what life is about? Being curious and learning about history and pertinent facts and information on a wide array of topics and, in the process, growing and evolving as a person?

If being *woke* means that I am curious and want to learn and, in the process, grow as a more informed human being, please count me in. I will embrace the term with pride. And if I am curious about the history, impacts and issues relating to race, justice, and equity and how we might, as a society, mitigate the negative impacts associated with those issues, by all means, please call me woke.

I am okay with being woke.

How about you?

# CHAPTER THIRTY-SEVEN

# FLIPPING THE SCRIPT

*"You can't understand someone until you have walked a mile in their shoes."*

—Anonymous

O nce again, let's be clear. Race is a social construct.

As discussed in Chapter Thirteen, a social construct is a concept or perception based on the collective views developed and maintained by a society or social group as opposed to existing inherently or naturally. It is a belief or concept created out of thin air.

So, let's rewrite some false history.

We're going to go back in time and flip the script. In our minds we are going to reconstruct our entire history of racism and discrimination against Blacks, from slavery to Jim Crow to mass incarceration, bans on voting, lynching, educational discrimination, medical sterilization, and the countless other ways in which Blacks Americans have been discriminated against for over 400 years.

And as we replay these events, we are going to change one part of that history. Rather than Blacks being considered the inferior race and subjected to these abhorrent practices, let's use an alternative social construct. Let's cast Whites as inferior and Blacks with all the power, privilege, and resources to write all the rules. Let's look back in history through the lens of this different social construct and relive every lynching, beating, unwarranted arrest, unjust prison sentence, and discriminatory policy, and rather than a Black person on the receiving end of those brutal and discriminatory practices, let's imagine a White person on the receiving end. Let's imagine walking a few miles in the shoes of Black Americans.

This begs the question. If in fact we had to walk a mile in a Black person's shoes, what would us Old White Dudes think?

How would we feel?

How would we react?

What would we do?

Ponder it.

# CHAPTER THIRTY-EIGHT

# OUR CHILDREN AND HOPE FOR THE FUTURE

*"Children are the world's most valuable resource and its best hope for the future."*

—John F. Kennedy

Children are not racist. At least not until they are taught to be racist. And just as racism can be taught, it can also be untaught. Through acceptance of responsibility, education, and effort it can be unlearned.

Our challenge is to teach our children compassion, understanding, justice, and equity as opposed to lessons of fear and persecution. In this sense, our efforts must start in the home.

Our children are our future, and what we say to or around them is vital. Kids pay attention to how their parents act. Little ears hear more than we think. We often say that "Oh, racism is going to gradually disappear because our children have lived in a much more diverse world." That is a weak excuse, for it allows us OWDs to feel we don't have to do anything because our children will take care of it for us. But on the other hand, there is some truth to that. Our children are our future, and it is on us to help prepare them to successfully meet future challenges.

Once again, James Baldwin from *The Fire Next Time*. "Color is not a human or personal reality; it is a political reality. But this is a distinction so extremely hard to make that the West has not been able to make it yet. And at the center of this dreadful storm, this vast confusion, stand the black people of this nation, who must now share the fate of a nation that has never accepted them, to which they were brought in chains. Well, if this is so, one has no choice but to do all in one's power to change that fate, and at no matter what risk—eviction, imprisonment, torture, death. For the sake of one's children, in order to minimize the bill *they* must pay, one must be careful not to take refuge in any delusion—and the value placed on the color of the skin is always and everywhere and forever, a delusion." (Baldwin 1992, 1993, 104)

In the end, it's about taking a leap of faith. We must have faith and trust that most people are good, honest, thoughtful, fair, caring, and community minded. People want to do and be a part of good and just things. We must trust them to reveal their inner kindness and commitment to those principles.

In Chapter One, I mentioned MFE's Keys for the City program and how since 2010, we have placed almost 200 pianos on the streets and how, over the course of fourteen years, we have experienced only two incidents of vandalism. I return to Keys for the City because the lesson learned through this experience was that until people prove otherwise, we should trust their better angels. People want to do the right thing. Sometimes, they simply need to be pointed in the right direction and encouraged to follow those instincts. The same holds true for issues around social justice. We must trust in people's better angels and that, given the education and opportunity, more people than you think will do the right thing.

While Darryl Davis may say otherwise, there are always going to be a certain percentage who are unreachable. But ample evidence exists to suggest that future generations provide hope. Consider how often you have witnessed groups of friends attend events or simply walk down the street and see people of all backgrounds and colors interacting, dating, working, or hanging out together. It is infinitely more than what most of us saw growing up. That feels like progress. It feels as if this is an example of the simmer stage in my Theory of Gumbo, which will be presented in full in Appendix A. When a diverse group of people (spices) mix and intermingle, it presents opportunities to build cross cultural understanding and relationships. The result is more ingredients mixing around together; Black, White, Hispanic/Latino, AAPI, LGBTQ+ and more. More ingredients make for a richer, better gumbo and a more integrated and just society.

This suggests we have the potential to become more equipped and inclined to recognize and respect everyone's basic humanity. Rather than wield our differences as a cudgel to divide us, we must offer the grace and empathy necessary to embrace our commonalities. At the end of the day, we have far more in common than we do differences.

Wendell Berry, in his book *The Hidden Wound*, touches on what might encourage and inspire someone to positively change their attitudes and behavior around issues of race.

"There is, I am sure, such a thing as a sense of guilt about historical wrongs, but I have the strongest doubts about the usefulness of a guilty conscious as a motivation: a man, I think, can be much more dependably motivated by a sense of what would be desirable than by a sense of what has been deplorable." (Berry 2010, 62)

We must be able to imagine a better future, a future that is more just. We must envision it because it provides a goal, vision, and something to work towards. It's not only about recognizing our past sins, but also about envisioning a better future. The question is what role do you want to play in creating that better future?

# CHAPTER THIRTY-NINE

## VOICES TO BE HEARD

*"Truth never damages a cause that is just."*

—Mahatma Gandhi

B e honest. How often do you talk to POC in any meaningful way? While you might have interactions with Black folk in some of your daily routines, how often do you engage in meaningful discussions of matters relating to race? Very rarely, I'd imagine. Again, I am not pointing fingers because I have been in the same boat.

My guess would be that, like most OWDs, we prefer to avoid the uncomfortable topic of racism. When confronted or challenged on these issues, our first reaction is to withdraw into silence, reflexively defend ourselves, or simply dismiss those voices as being overly reactive. And who wants to take the chance of getting people riled up? But in willfully ignoring or dismissing those voices, we cannot hear, let alone understand, the real issues POC face every day.

When thinking about what can be done to disrupt racism, let's turn again to Robin DiAngelo. She offers what might be the most basic action we can take. We can listen. She writes about conducting diversity training workshops during which she asks POC, "How often have you given white people feedback on our unaware yet inevitable racism? How often has that gone well for you?"

She explains the reaction of POC to that question. "Eye-rolling, head-shaking, and outright laughter follow, along with the consensus of *rarely, if ever.* I then ask, 'What would it feel like if you could simply give us feedback, have us graciously receive it, reflect, and work to change the behavior?' Recently, a man of color sighed and said, 'It would be revolutionary.' I ask my fellow whites to consider the profundity of that response. It would be *revolutionary* if we could receive, reflect, and work to change the behavior. On the one hand, the man's response points to how difficult and fragile we are. But on the other hand, it indicates how simple it can be to take responsibility for our racism. However, we aren't likely to get there if we are operating from the dominant worldview that only intentionally mean people can participate in racism." (White Fragility, 113)

At a minimum, we can listen with grace and humility.

The purpose of this chapter is to provide an opportunity for some POC to speak their mind regarding their realities of living in a world of systemic racism. Given that we know little about those realities, it is an opportunity to expand our understanding. To that end, I asked nine POC, most of whom I met through the SFJ project, to write a short passage of about 500 words in answer to these questions:

"What would you say to White people regarding racism, justice and equity? What message, points or observations would you offer"?

My hope in providing this opportunity to speak directly to us on the realities POC face every day will be informative and beneficial. In so doing, I had a major decision to make. Specifically, whether there was a need to place a caveat on those comments. Should the contributors be encouraged not to be too divisive, accusatory, or aggressive in their comments? If the comments came across as being too angry, would us OWDs be offended and thus unable to consider their viewpoints? Would our tendency to retreat to our standard posture of White fragility render the exercise fruitless?

The work titled *Me and White Supremacy: Combat Racism, Change the World, and Become a Good Ancestor* by Layla F. Saad, outlines a step-by-step reflection process to encourage us to examine our White privilege and racist behaviors. It is a wonderful and utilitarian tome, with thoughtful and challenging exercises and discussion questions. She talks about *tone policing,* which she describes as, "A tactic used by those who have privilege to silence those who do not by focusing on the tone of what is being said rather than the actual content."

She goes on to offer examples of tone policing by Whites:

- "I wish you would say what you're saying in a nicer way.
- I can't take in what you're telling me about your lived experiences because you sound too angry.
- You should address white people in a more civil way if you want us to join your cause.
- The way you are talking about this issue is not productive.
- You are bringing too much negativity into this space, and you should focus on progress." (Pp. 50 – 51)

She adds how tone policing reinforces White supremacist norms of how POC are supposed to show up. "It is a way of keeping BIPOC in line and disempowered. When you insist that you will not believe or give credibility or attention to BIPOC until they speak in a tone that suits you, then you uphold the idea that your standards as a White person are more superior. When you control the tone of how BIPOC are supposed to talk about their lived experiences with racism and existing in the world, you are reinforcing the white supremist ideology that white knows best." (P. 50)

She continues. "When you insist that BIPOC talk about their painful experiences with racism without expressing any pain, rage, or grief, you are asking them to dehumanize themselves. Tone policing is both a request that BIPOC share our experiences about racism without sharing any of our (real) emotions about it and for us to exist in ways that do not make white people feel uncomfortable." (51)

It was fortuitous to have read Saad's book before setting parameters on what contributors wrote or how they chose to express it. In doing so, I would have been tone policing. This illustrates the benefits of doing the work. I would have never realized how disrespectful and tone deaf it would have been to put parameters on how they should tell their stories to protect my White fragility had I not done the work. Doing the work revealed to me that if I was serious about providing an honest platform for POC to say something meaningful, I needed to throw White fragility in the dumpster. I needed to create an open platform.

While learning about tone policing was an important lesson, there was another enlightening lesson I learned when working on the specifics of this chapter. It was an unexpected lesson that once again, showed how clueless us White folks can be when it comes to racism and equity. While I was exposed to a slice of the issue in my reading and research, I must, once again, thank Tony Collins for bringing the issue to my attention in a clear, illuminating, and powerful way.

Tony caused me to realize that in conceptualizing and implementing my plan for this chapter I did something White folks have done forever and continue to do all too often. Specifically, I asked POC to elaborate on racism in America. The problem, however, is that I asked them to do that without compensation. They are providing something that is extremely valuable, yet I did not offer an honorarium recognizing their contribution. To not do so was disrespectful of their perspective and lived experiences. As I have come to learn, this is another example of an OWD asking POC for free labor.

Here's something else I was completely clueless about. What I had neither an understanding of nor appreciation for is that when POC are asked to opine on these issues, they are required to relive all the hate, pain, fear, discrimination, and rejection they have experienced throughout their lifetime because of systemic racism. I simply did not consider how extremely traumatic that must be. When Tony pointed this out to me, it hit me in the forehead like a ton of bricks.

Another lesson learned.

Considering that new understanding, I attempted to rectify this oversight by offering each of the contributors a small honorarium for their essays. While that small honorarium was certainly not reflective of the value of their contribution, it was, at least a recognition of their effort.

While you hate to make mistakes, and I have made many on this journey, making a mistake is also an opportunity to learn and grow. It also provided an opportunity for me to recognize and appreciate the space and grace these contributors, as well as other POC, provided me to make mistakes on my journey, learn from them and move forward to continue the work.

In short, it is critical that we provide space for POC to tell their stories because their stories, like ours, are American stories. And because we have little idea what it means to be a POC in America, we should listen with respect, empathy, and humility. Again, I am not pointing fingers. I'm on the same journey and need to educate myself on that history by listening to the stories, narratives, and perspectives of the voices of those who have lived that experience. It's time for us OWD's to be revolutionary.

Here is what they said.

## LE HINTON

"Much of what I've learned in this long, brief life, I've learned through patience and listening. In order to do that I have to stop talking, be quiet, fall silent, and simply shut up. In a world where everyone has an opinion, where everyone is encouraged to express said opinion, it is rare to find people who are content to receive information and not want to interject their opinion or point of view. But that's not how one learns.

"When I was in first grade, our teacher taught us how to count to ten in German. My aunt happened to be from Germany and lived there until she met and married my uncle and moved to the States. She taught us some words of German: *danke, bitte,* and a few more. If, in first grade I'd blurted out how much I knew because of my aunt, besides getting into trouble, I wouldn't have learned to count in German. I needed to be quiet, to listen, then process what I heard. Even at six-years-old I knew that is how one learns. A little experience in an area doesn't translate to complete knowledge.

"For whites regarding racism, I say be quiet, listen, and process all that is said by people of color about racism and their experiences.

Remember, in this area, you don't have an opinion. Your experience isn't germane to the discussion. In the same way that my tiny German vocabulary was not pertinent in 1$^{st}$ grade, your interactions with Jamal at work are merely side notes that you should put aside while listening to everything you can about the experiences of people of color with racism, justice, and equity. Please don't offer an alternative reason for why the security guard may have walked past five groups of young white men playing basketball in the college's gym before asking the only group of young black men for their college ids. Just listen first and absorb his memory. Absorb the information. Absorb his realization from 50 years ago that black people being intelligent, working hard, and applying themselves are not even close to being the keys to racial harmony."

Just be quiet. Just listen. Just absorb the information and pain. We can start there.

**Le Hinton** is an African American, Buddhist poet whose sensibilities were partially shaped by his baby boomer generation. On the evening of April 4, 1968, he went to his room and cried the rest of the night. That evening placed a ceiling on his general optimism. Later, his Buddhist studies raised that ceiling, but the ceiling remains. He has hope that the ceiling will someday open to the sky.

## DR. LEROY HOPKINS

"Racism vs discrimination. On the surface they seem like two sides of the same coin. However, racism requires either the force of law or individual action directed against another party. Discrimination is a general tendency which can develop in confrontations with persons, attitudes, and concepts that differ from one's own training and experience. Past racial practices do, however, influence contemporary discrimination. That is the case here in Lancaster. If one wishes a gauge of racism in its historical dimension locally, it is only necessary to look at a newspaper from the 19$^{th}$ century.

"Besides a complete palette of racial epithets, 19$^{th}$ century Lancaster newspapers describe in vivid detail local Blacks as parasites and morally depraved individuals whose very existence is blight on proper society. Pre-Civil War, amalgamation, the mixing of the races was generally decried as an ever-present danger to a healthy society. As was the case elsewhere before 1860 this racial animosity erupted into racial attacks (the Columbia Race Riots of 1834/1835). Those uprisings were directed against Blacks who, in the view of the rioters, entered an area where they were unwanted because of their race: the local economy.

"After 1900 the first serious racial conflicts arose out of the protests run by the Lancaster Chapter of the NAACP in downtown Lancaster and at Rocky Springs Amusement Park in the Summer of 1963. Characteristically, the local reaction to the protests were that they were the result of outside agitators. Local Blacks were presumably satisfied with low-income jobs, substandard housing, and low educational attainment. To quell this grassroots effort to change the racial landscape an Urban League affiliate was organized because that organization was known for working within the establishment and not challenging it from the outside. And there we have the local racial situation in a nutshell.

"Local whites feel entitled to decide who can succeed or fail. Some groups have become upset by advancements accrued to the Black community by the passage of new laws or because of personal initiative. That is why the voting process needs to be reviewed and white supremacist groups are active here. There is an underlying fear that white privilege is at stake. What does white privilege look like locally? Blacks have historically had difficulty obtaining vocational training, securing financing for either a mortgage or a business start-up, and by and large local policy makers in government and the private sector are neither Black nor Brown. The fight to address these inequities resulted in Affirmative Action laws which provided a path to careers not for local persons, but individuals recruited from elsewhere.

"The challenge for the future because of changing demographics, which before the end of this century will likely find our area majority minority, is whether society can overcome discriminatory practices grounded in yesterday's racial attitudes and move to a more inclusive society in which individuals are encouraged to develop their skills and not merely subside as a dependent of an indifferent society."

**Dr. Hopkins** attended the Lancaster city school system before matriculating to Millersville State College where he earned a bachelor's degree in German and Russian. He attended Harvard University where he earned a PhD in Germanic languages and Literature. After a teaching stint in Germany, he returned to Lancaster as associate director for program and planning for the Lancaster Urban League, eventually being appointed as interim executive director. He also served as assistant professor of German at Millersville University, and retired with emeritus status. He has served on several non-profit boards including Lancaster History, Crispus Attucks Center, The Martin Luther King Breakfast committee as well as president of the African American Historical Society of South-Central Pennylvania. He continues to research about African American life in Lancaster County.

## MADISON DEWISPELAERE

"What would I say to white people regarding racism, justice and equity? As I reflect on this question, I cannot help but think, who am I? I am a white-passing non-Spanish speaking Hispanic, so who am I to speak on issues of racism, justice and equity? Issues that I have never been able to fully, deeply understand due to my privilege as a white-passing Puerto Rican. For the majority of my life, I have always felt like an 'in-betweener' a person who never fully fit into any particular category or felt fully accepted by the various identities that I hold. Growing up, I was considered to be the 'white' one of my family but at my predominantly white school, I was often asked if I was Black because of how dark I would get in the summertime or because of how frizzy my curls were compared to my silky-haired white friends. I was frequently told that I looked 'so much better with straightened hair' and I even had a guy once tell me that I shouldn't get too tan in the summer because I looked 'ugly.' In short, it was obvious that I was not white.

"I felt for a very long time that I did not belong anywhere, that I was neither Hispanic nor white, a feeling that resonates with a lot of multi-racial and multi-cultural individuals. Despite my struggle with identity, I saw first-hand racism and discrimination by predominantly white peers I grew up surrounded by but I even saw blatant colorism within my own Hispanic family as being 'light-skinned' was deemed more desirable. If there is anything that I have learned from my experience as a multi-racial woman, it's that we are all multi-dimensional beings, not meant to be placed into a box or slapped with a label. All of us, even white people. You would probably be pretty annoyed if you were only identified as 'the guy who wears khakis,' knowing full well that you have a full wardrobe at home. This example sounds ridiculous, I know, but that's how ridiculous it sounds when POC are only referred to by the color of their skin instead of the multi-faceted people that we are.

"We are all things that encompass us, the nuances of our being that permeate our relationships, communities, professions, lives. We do ourselves a disservice by placing labels on individuals or leading with bias, especially if we are solely developing perceptions based on somebody's skin tone or culture.

"So, if I were to revisit this question again, what would I say to white people? I would say that we must look beyond the surface-level labels. Peel back the layers. Dive deeper. Find the connection points with people that you otherwise would not have taken the time to do. You might surprise yourself at how much you reveal about your own identity by unlocking more about others.

"Also, quit telling Black and Brown women that they look better with straight hair."

**Madison DeWispelaere** is a recent graduate of Villanova University and Founder of Obsidian Media Haus.

## FRAN RODRIGUEZ

"Born and raised in Brooklyn (1963). Youngest of 7. First to attend and graduate from college. My transient life in Lancaster began during the 1970's, creating a love-hate relationship with this place I now call home.

Guess what? I've never felt a sense of belonging here and have experienced harsh, debilitating moments of racism, mostly from white men.

"Being tokenized as the only woman of color throughout my career and community involvement for many years created trauma I'm still working through in therapy. And yet, my contributions to the Red Rose city have remained relentless for 3 decades strong.

"As an activist in the early 2000's, my focus was all about organizing and engaging the masses to get involved. Fast forward to 2022. As a Black Puerto Rican and elder, I now have the responsibility and luxury of deciding which systems of oppression to disrupt wherever necessary.

"White folks, here's my gift to you:

1. **Minority/Disadvantaged**—Please stop using these words to describe the BIPOC community. Remove them from your vocabulary immediately.

2. **Your brain**—"Let's get together. I'd like to pick your brain about something I'm working on" – When BIPOC receive this invitation from a white person, it's a red flag.

3. **I see you**—Nothing is more dehumanizing than ignoring Black women at meetings or events, especially during conversations that involve them. Make eye contact.

4. **Stereotypes**—Latinx are not a monolith! We represent 20 different countries. Also, "Hispanic" and "Latinx" are not a race; nor are they interchangeable.

5. **365**—Black history should be celebrated <u>every single day</u> of the year. Don't wait until February.

6. **Nothing about us without us**—If you're creating programming for the BIPOC community, our people should plan, implement, and deliver it, and don't forget to pay us!

7. **Lived experience**— BIPOC with valuable lived experience are often overlooked from opportunities. Don't always look for academic credentials.

8. **Bragging rights**—If you've created multiple anti-racism and equity programs or read 100 books by Black authors, be sure to tell your white colleagues/friends. Encourage them to do the same. There's no need to brag about these things to BIPOC. It's annoying.

9. **The table**—Before inviting us to your board/committee/organization/company, do the internal work first and then make room at the table. In other words, please stop causing harm by tokenizing us.

10. **Winning**—When BIPOC win, the entire community wins!"

**Fran Rodriguez** is a visionary strategist who thrives at creating community-led initiatives with one mission—to empower people and disrupt the status quo! She currently serves as board chair of LEAD PA Institute, a nonpartisan statewide organization cultivating Pennsylvania's progressive and civic leaders seeking to serve in elected office or advocacy roles. Fran holds an associate's of degree in paralegal studies from HACC, and a master's in Human Services from Lincoln University.

## AMY BANKS

"Dear White People:

"If you want to have a meaningful discussion about race and inequity in this country, don't expect me to teach you. And don't think that asking about my 'experience' as a black woman in this country is opening a dialogue. If you can't understand what I speak of without me having to describe it to you, you haven't done your homework. And by homework, I mean, studying about the history of slavery, emancipation, reconstruction, the Jim Crow south, the Great Migration and learn up about institutionalized policies—from denial of education, healthcare, and wealth-building tools of any kind—to redlining, and policing. After that, take a look at your history and life choices, and identify where you benefited from being white. Then you can ask me a meaningful question and I might be able to tell you about how systemic racism impacted me. Look in your life where possible assumptions and attitudes that reside in you and tell me about them. Then ask me how my experience socializing while growing up, or getting jobs or determining what I wanted to do when I grew up was impacted by the color of my skin and racism.

"I might be able to have a conversation that was generated from thoughtful research and self-reflection. But I might not. Because, really, I don't trust you. I won't trust your motivation and will likely suspect that you are trying to minimize your collusion and the benefit you gained from it, or mitigate your guilt, or get in my pants. And that's okay, too. You need to be okay with my distrust of you, even the 'peace-loving liberals.' The grievance is egregious, and even the high-yella, educated, white-talking black folks have navigated the slings and arrows of racism in the United States. We all have scars from the injustice, (and so do whites,) because racism has no boundaries. It is a toxin in the air we breathe.

"So, good luck.

"I am a black woman born of a white woman and a black man. In the year of my birth, interracial marriage was legal in eleven of these 50 united states. Raised in Minnesota in a white, middle-class neighborhood, by parents far from their own family roots, my brother and I were brought up in an unhappy household by people quite unaware of the trauma inflicted upon their bodies and psyche simply from choosing to marry and have children. Not to mention the added traumas of poverty, losing a mother at an early age, and emotional abuse. And, being black. (For my father, of course.)

"It wasn't until I moved to Atlanta, Georgia, (amid the perception that the south was full of men in white sheets and hoods, chasing and doing horrible things to the black people,) that I came to understand the totality of the racism I endured growing up with the Minnesota Nice. Though it took about five years to overcome the culture shock, Atlanta taught me Black Pride and Community. At Agnes Scott College, my Women and Religion professor, (a tiny young white woman,) Dr. Tina Pippin introduced me to the concept of white privilege. From there, my eyes were opened, and I finally started to put words to the experience. A new wave of self-identifying has occurred since 2020 and if I sound at all angry in this commentary, it is because I am.

**Amy Banks** was brought up in the North, schooled in the South, and has called the East Coast home for most of her adult life. A career singer and entertainer, she spends most of her working day in arts communication for a local university. Amy has been Black her entire life.

## TERIAN MACK

"I was born in Lancaster, Pennsylvania into a biracial family. My mom is white and my dad is from Panama, the first generation from his side born in the US. I am now the father of two children.

"I grew up loving music before even really having an understanding of what it was. As a child, I'd dance and sing to 90s hip-hop and rap songs. When I found out that most of what I was hearing started as words on paper, I had enough inspiration for a lifetime. I was also an obsessive sketch artist and loved the imagery and emotion I could sketch with my words. As I began writing poems and raps that eventually turned into songs years later, I realized the true power of this art form. Before ever performing or holding a mic, I knew that when my time came to put my words and raps to music and beats, I would have a message to deliver. Since then, I've dedicated myself to rapping for a purpose. By letting people know my purpose, I hope to inspire others to find theirs. I started performing live in front of small crowds, expressing myself and my message. People not only need music but our communities need art and music to help us progress along as a village. Art and music bring us together. Through my volunteer work in schools, I've seen an overflow of students who are creators and artists who need to see that their future can be whatever they dream. Music's power can be life changing in that regard.

"But there seems to be a disconnect between what people think hip-hop/rap is and what it actually is. We, the Black community, use rap as an outlet. It's therapy for us to use emotion and words to express what we see and experience. A band that has beautiful music and musicians in suits and ties who write their music in their home studio with a coffee while their kids are at school and his wife is busy shopping has the EXACT same power and process as a 'rapper.' Both putting their experience, life, and emotion into song, playing it live publicly to connect to those who understand and value their craft.

"Hip-hop and rap is now the number one genre in the world, generating the largest amount of revenue in the music and entertainment industry. Yes, there is rap and hip-hop that isn't necessarily beneficial for kids to hear, but that's in any entertainment medium. We all hear rap and hip-hop on the radio daily. It's normal.

"Recently, during a live public performance, the police threatened to shut down the show and give out fines if we didn't follow his orders. He asked that we don't use profanity or say inappropriate lyrics but it was in a very authoritarian manor that was out of place in such a positive setting. He didn't give the performers his attention, listen to the music or even notice the crowd was full of families and kids. He didn't take time to notice there was no cussing and that the music was being enjoyed by everyone of all ages and backgrounds. Shutting down a show because of what they THINK is hip-hop or rap shows the disconnect between the people who understand and respect the art form and those who don't. Unfortunately, race plays a factor in this because they see a stage and crowd of Black and Brown men and women and assume the music isn't fit for the community.

"Maybe the officer wasn't racist or prejudice. Maybe he was just ignorant to the true power of good music."

**Terian Mack:** A brilliant songwriter, painter, recording artist, father of two, and entrepreneur with a story of triumph and persistence, Lancaster's own Terian Mack's humble beginnings speak to the underdog in us all. Terian is currently working with record label and advertising agency UnitedMasters/Translation, based out of Brooklyn,

New York. We have a lot to look forward to from this forecasted star as he merges education, art, and community with a purpose.

## TONY COLLINS

"I no longer believe that 'white people,' at least most of them, actually give a damn about racism, justice or equity. I'm not simply referring to the overtly racist and fascist. Their point of view is all too obvious. I'm talking about the 'busy middle,' white Americans that watch while the zealots attempt to resurrect the pre-civil rights era and don't understand why Black Americans are angry. For them, working on social justice is too difficult. It might require them to be uncomfortable, to change direction or relinquish privileges. My recent experiences have convinced me that it is rare for a white person to ponder racism and its roots. That type of reflection is reserved for Black History Month, Martin Luther King's birthday or when a catastrophic event like the murder of George Floyd is in the news, then quickly abandoned as the next holiday approaches or current events present another crisis.

"Black people are always asked to opine on the nature of racism. It is bad enough that they are seldom paid for this work of education but there seems to be very little understanding that asking Black people about racism is also asking them to relive every moment of pain, fear, or rejection experienced in their daily lives-for the entertainment of a white audience. A white audience that is perfectly comfortable denying that any of these moments are racism while they implore us to not make everything about race. It is exhausting and demoralizing.

"Today significant numbers of white America are publicly committed to returning the country to the bad old days, revealed in a concerted effort to restrict voting rights, eliminate conversations about race and create a story about America that has no relationship to the truth. There is a full-throated effort to present a version of American history that denies inflicting a genocide on Native Americans, reinvents the story of slavery, and suggest talking about equity is anti-Christian.

Then, I was reminded by Bryan Stevenson, 'We must remain hopeful, it is our superpower. We are going to have to do uncomfortable things.' In this moment, talking about racism to white people is uncomfortable but it is something that must be done.

"Being white in American means never being afraid if you're stopped by police after dark. It means being presumed innocent if there is a confrontation between people of different colors. It means having technology designed to reflect your pigmentation in public places. It means being assumed to be an eligible voter no matter how you show up at the polls. It means being believed by doctors when you say you are in pain. It means being assumed innocent as you are assaulting someone of color on a video.

"Problems of racial justice are for whites to resolve, and they won't make any progress until they are willing to forgo their comforts. White people need to reflect on their privilege and be willing to adjust their world view. Adjusting their world view must include a reconstruction of their understanding of American history. And it will require interacting with people of color who are willing to speak the truth even if it means the conversation is uncomfortable. There cannot be progress toward racial justice until the white power structure and the communities of color develop the mental toughness and trust to consider the truth together."

**Tony Collins:** President of Blake Collins Group, Tony is a seasoned public relations professional with a unique combination of public sector and business development expertise. A Senior Vice President of Florida public relations firm Tucker/Hall for thirteen years, he worked with corporations, government agencies, non-government agencies and non-profits throughout Florida as a public affairs and communications strategist.

## KEVIN RESSLER

"I must begin with the disclosure that John Gerdy is a personal friend. We don't get together much often, in fact it is barely at all. But here's what I know about my friendship with John. When I have a worry, a concern, or a need to better understand confounding perspectives that come my way in my line of work from other white men of his age, John picks up the phone or meets up with me somewhere and we can work through it together. In those same instances or circumstances where John is the one confounded by the actions of others around issues of justice it is known that I will pick up the phone or meet him out.

"I'm not an old white dude, depending on who you ask 38 isn't really even that old. But we need allies to bolster and support us when our appeals for equity and fairness in the treatment of people who look like me are met with senseless rejection or accusations of partisanship and politicization. I'm an optimist, I believe that people are always well intentioned and fair until they prove me otherwise. The world doesn't quite work like that, and people like John who have been in the rooms of decision makers that impact the futures of black student athletes, marginalized schools and their student artists, or other institutions are there to help remind me of the sobering realities without demeaning my desired optimism.

"For those of us who have done this 'justice' work our whole lives, we can also become jaded and even despondent amidst our aspirational optimism. Because it's just not fair that the load is constantly carried against frequent opposition of those who are so pearl clutching of their advantages that fairness is a zero-sum game by the shoulders of individuals for whom the disenfranchisement is borne. This book isn't perfect, no book is, but this book endeavors. Even in the process of communication about this essay, John has demonstrated his learnings in the process and improved how he asked myself and others to write something.

"Look, you're not going to agree with everything in the book. I don't agree with everything in the book. Here's the common ground: nobody ever got anywhere alone. Wipe from your mind the belief that those who don't have what you have didn't work as hard as you did. Wipe from your mind the belief that the value of a person is in what they have been able to accumulate. Wipe from your mind that there is even in anyway inherent differences in value. We have all been socialized with a bunch of junk social sciences and opinions around 'other' people. We are the same. That is not the same as saying we have the same opportunities or the world is constructed in some kind of way where there is equity. There's too much history to not look at the world and say, 'I have nothing to learn' and yet so many of us stop learning the important introspective and philosophical lessons when we are a teenager. We move to task, to skill, to production education and we forget about the humanity of our very existence.

"This book is necessary. Not because John, an old white dude, has something to teach and we the class need to sit and study. This book is necessary because it is one guy, John, who is willing to say (that even as old as he is, and even amidst the perspectives formed and shaped by the external interactions influenced by his being white, and even with the accomplishments he can rest upon) . . . I yet grow. This book is necessary because it's an example of a book you can write: "An *(insert age) (insert identifying demographic)'s* thoughts on people society treats differently."

**Kevin Ressler** has spent his life seeking ways to bring about an equitable peace and justice for all. He earned a master's of divinity through Lancaster Theological Seminary, hoping to integrate his spiritual and moral concerns with the professional activities he could engage through non-profit leadership. He spent five years growing Meals on Wheel of Lancaster and on January 1, 2020, assumed the role of president and CEO of United Way of Lancaster County.

## SIR DOMINIQUE JORDAN, THE PROLIFIC ONE

"I begin with a poem:

### What's your revolution?
*Imma keep moving,*
*I don't really need music,*
*I just use it as a tool to reach those that are clueless*

*About are YOUTH feeling useless,*
*To elude any doom,*
*WE must choose to be glue,*
*Come together to improve this,*
*Situation that consumes us,*
*Imma prude to the limits set upon us by the ruthless*
*What's your revolution?!*

"A magnetic juxtaposition it is to attempt to lead young rebels stepping into their purpose; rather than allowing them to flourish with the utmost support after cultivating the courage it takes to even stand against a system built to rid away the potential of the marginalized. What if John Brown stepped aside to allow former enslaved persons to liberate themselves in a manner they deemed fit, rather than them being a part of a forgotten army of another white martyr. What would that have done for History? Not saying there isn't space for us all to fight against racial oppression, but the guise of an ally or even a co-conspirator without first recognizing how your privilege can and often reminds not just BIPOC, but more specifically, Black people of how much farther we have to overcome is blatantly disrespectful.

"It seems that being advised by older white men on how to counteract a collapsing society that was created by older white men is inevitable. The issues I have with this leaves me with a paradox, *why is a revolving door always closed?* The drafty winds of turmoil and karma are left outside for the majority of us to deal with, while one or a few of the good ones just may be allowed in the room to represent in some pretentious facet. Don't just give us the floor to speak or the room to stand in, that's not justice... more so the access to develop our own sound choices to make an intentional mark on our communities.

"Black Lives Matter is not a slogan, nor a political agenda, but a way of life! We finally live in a time where being unapologetic about blackness just might get us a quarter of that American dream, or even our supposed 40 acres, at least while it is in style. What happens when it isn't anymore?

"We demand access to the resources that are put in place to help further our people, yet we still have been waiting with our hands out for an opportunity to present itself. Raw Creativity as I like to call, Artivism, from those that yearn for a better day, could, should, and will inspire, enlighten, then activate the leaders we were destined to become, we just need YOU to step aside as a guide and give grace as we walk in faith and fortitude. In conclusion, I challenge those reading this to think outside the box, use your influence to the best of your ability to amplify those desperately deserving to tell their own story…

What That Impact Do!"

**Sir Dominique Jordan, The Prolific One** is a poetic vanguard hailing from Lancaster, Pennsylvania. Whether in spoken word or on a page, he uses his unique verbiage to inspire others to use their vulnerability as a super power. He identifies as an *artivist,* and teaches across the country about how hip-hop culture and general creative expression are tools that can be used in the classroom/neighborhood to enhance the overall educational experience. He loves to challenge people to make a difference in their community as they see fit. You can find him and his efforts on social media using the hashtag #WhatThatImpactD

# CHAPTER FORTY

## LET'S GET ON IT!

*"Do the best you can until you know better. Then when you know better, do better."*

—Maya Angelou

As mentioned, I believe in people's better angels. Most people want to do the right thing and be a positive force in our society. The challenge is to provide them the information, inspiration, encouragement, and support to take that first step to do something to make a difference.

It's easy to deny responsibility, shift blame, or bury your head in the sand because addressing racial justice issues is fraught and challenging. That said, it's no longer enough to simply talk about justice and equity. It's time to act in some way, big or small. To make an effort. To figure out a way to be an active part of the solution. That doesn't mean you must go all Mother Teresa and change the world. There was only one Mother Teresa. But there is also only one you. Because you are unique you can, in your own way, change the world. And if not the world, perhaps your town, or your neighborhood, or your block or your family. Martin Luther King summed it up well. "If I cannot do great things, I can do small things in great ways." (GoodReads.com) In other words, we've got to get on this. We've got to challenge ourselves to do something. Returning to basketball and where this journey began, we've got to get to the scorer's table and check ourselves into the game.

There are many things we can do to contribute to the cause. But, as mentioned, the first step of making a conscious decision to act on those convictions is critical. Once you take that step, you will begin to discover ways in which you can adjust your priorities, behaviors, and actions around these issues.

Le Hinton is a teacher, lecturer, and author of six poetry collections. We were fortunate that he contributed a poem for Volume One of the SFJ series titled "Until We're Not." He also contributed an essay for the "Voices to be Heard" chapter of this book. As part of the public release of each record, we also produce a webinar that features the various contributors to the record, from the musician to the visual artist to the reader of the speech to a representative of the featured CBO. During the webinar we discuss issues around social justice as well as their inspiration behind their contributions and their perceptions of the role and responsibilities of artists and musicians as it applies to bearing witness around issues of justice and equity. We also ask them to provide examples of things large and small that we can do to contribute to the fight against racism and injustice.

Le is a thoughtful man who exudes decency and compassion. He offered a basic action we can all take as a starting point. He suggested that, at a minimum, we engage with people. We say hello and perhaps compliment them or say something to elicit a smile. He talked about there being so many *invisible people* who we simply do not acknowledge, even in a casual way. When Le spoke of this he reminded me of my mother. She also talked about the importance of acknowledging another person's existence and basic humanity. Perhaps that is a small item, but it's an important start. And it's something that you can do by simply opening your heart to other human beings. Simple yet profound.

Words, and how and where you use them, also matter. Don't underestimate the power of your voice. What you say matters. You never know who is listening. Ears, young and old, are everywhere. Pay attention to the words and language you use. The fact that others are listening presents an opportunity to spread the word. These are the basics. They are things that everyone can do. And you can do more by raising your voice to challenge and educate, including family and friends, when they make a racist remark or espouse a false or harmful narrative around race.

If interested, you can go beyond those basics in ways that do not require an enormous amount of time and resources. Think about something that fits your resources, interests, and talents. Whether it's writing a check to support an organization working on issues related to social justice or volunteering at such an organization.

For some, it's easy to write a check. I am fortunate to be able to do a certain amount of that. And, as the executive director of a non-profit organization, I understand and appreciate that without those checks organizations can't do the good things they do. You cannot underestimate the importance of providing financial support for organizations that are doing good work around social justice. Given the challenges these organizations face and the magnitude of the issues they handle, every dollar counts.

This is another lesson learned through my personal journey to become a more effective contributor to the cause of social justice. Specifically, it has caused me to rethink my general charitable giving priorities. As a result, moving forward I am going to be more strategic and directed in giving to CBOs that are doing good work around issues of justice and equity.

But here's the interesting twist when it comes to supporting social justice causes as opposed to many other worthy non-profits. There are many non-profits to which you can write a check and be done with it. Consider for example a food bank, homeless shelter, or an arts organization. While those checks are enormously important and impactful, your personal commitment to and investment in those causes are, for the most part, limited. In other words, you write your check because you believe in the cause and leave it up to the organization to use it wisely. By writing that check, you have done your due diligence and a good thing because there are so many worthy causes that you can't fully immerse yourself in all of them. So, you do what you can.

Here's the difference when it comes to social justice causes and organizations. Your role in making a difference is not something that can be left entirely to the organization to address. Issues of social justice impact each of us in profound ways daily. Even if you financially support an organization that fights racism, you still must live your everyday life. And it's a life in which you encounter and interact with POC and can still, with no ill intent, engage in racist behaviors. In other words, there is a financial aspect to fighting racism, but there is also a personal behavioral aspect. Simply because you write a check does not excuse you from doing the behavioral things—acknowledging your White privilege, doing the research, and asking questions, as discussed in the previous pages.

The point is that the issues and challenges relating to social justice, equity, inclusion, racism, and human dignity have been baked into our families, neighborhoods, schools, legal and heath care systems, nation, and society for hundreds of years. Similar to a business writing a social justice statement and slapping a BLM sign in the window, it requires more. You still must acknowledge and confront these issues and the myriad of challenges they present on a daily basis.

Here's great news for those who want to do more. Because there are many organizations addressing issues around justice and equity, the opportunities to do something concrete with those organizations are vast. Organizations such as the NAACP have a focused mission around social justice. But there are many more non-profit organizations with missions not specifically about social or racial justice, but that are in fact, doing work on justice and equity issues. These organizations are necessary due to the harmful societal impacts of systemic racism. They include organizations that work to eradicate hunger or provide low-cost housing or educational opportunities or highlight criminal justice issues. While they might not be specific about it in their mission statements, they are, in fact, doing social justice and equity work, albeit in less direct and more nuanced ways. Surely you can identify a few, whether local or national, with organizational missions you can enthusiastically support.

The challenge is to be thoughtful, directed, and strategic in determining how to contribute. While that might seem daunting, the possibilities to act in meaningful ways are endless. It's like a jigsaw puzzle. There are many options and opportunities. The challenge is to piece them together in a way that makes you feel you are having an impact. You first assess your talents, interests, and resources, including time and money. You do the research to find out where the needs are, and which community groups and CBOs are working in a space or on a cause that can get you excited. Meet with them. Ask questions. Explore ways in which you might be able to help. Most non-profit organizations are stretched financially and understaffed and welcome volunteer help. The hardest part is taking that first step. It's a big one. But I promise that when you do you will not regret it. And the possibilities of where that first step might take you are endless.

Here's an example. One of my favorite CBOs is the Lancaster Early Education Center (LEEC). It has provided high quality day care for low-income families for over 100 years. What is so special about the LEEC is that to receive day care for their children, parents must either be working or in school and must actively participate in various classes or workshops on parenting and other family building initiatives. The LEEC is not a place to simply drop kids off for babysitting. It's a family centered community. I visited the executive director to express my interest in volunteering, and, as noted, because non-profit organizations are always looking for volunteers, was welcomed with open arms. They loved that I was a stay-at-home father. I offered a different, more diverse profile from other board members, who were overwhelmingly women. It sounded like a perfect fit. I was soon asked to be a board member, eventually serving as president of the board. I have since cycled off the board but remain involved at the LEEC where I periodically show up as Willie Marble to entertain the children with my participatory, blues-education sessions.

You never know what a particular non-profit might need. That's what makes the possibilities so vast. You may find yourself in a place where your skills, background, and interests match perfectly with the organization's needs. The potential in these synergies is enormous. But until you make the effort to take that first step, you will never find out how significant your impact might be.

What are your talents and interests? Are you a visual artist? Maybe you work with a local Boys and Girls Club to put together a group of kids to guide through the process of painting a mural in their neighborhood. Or perhaps you are a poet or like to write. My guess is that if you reach out to the right CBO, they will bend over backwards to create an opportunity for you to work with youth or adults teaching them poetry or creative writing. Or maybe you connect with a neighborhood group and put together a once-a-month beautification crew to pick up trash in the neighborhood. If you love gardening, why not identify an organization to partner with to put together a community garden? It can be as simple as volunteering to serve as an after-school tutor for one child once a week. It can be as big as you like and as involved as your schedule and passion allows. The possibilities are endless. The only barrier is a lack of imagination—and the fear of taking that first step.

Further, the opportunity to make your unique impact around justice and equity issues has never been greater for three reasons. First, since the George Floyd murder, awareness of, and interest in, these issues is particularly high. It's safe to say there are many people who want to contribute to the cause. That means you will likely have a host of allies who want to join hands to make a difference. So many people simply need a nudge to encourage them to check into the game.

Second, the tools at your disposal are numerous and effective. I will use Music For Everyone as an example. While I had a cause and was passionate about it, I knew nothing of how to build a non-profit organization. But here's what is so exciting about the birth, development, and growth of MFE. It relates to the amazing world of technology, communication, and social media. If we would have created MFE twenty-five years ago, we would have needed to work through an established *big box* (for lack of a better term) music focused non-profit. In Lancaster that would have been the Fulton Theater or the Lancaster Symphony. Those organizations had the heft in the form of contacts, mailing lists, facilities, staff, and influential board members to get MFE off the ground and running. But big organizations come with big bureaucracy. Lots of committees. All types of established policies and procedures. And decision processes that are often slow and difficult to navigate. We didn't have time for that. We wanted to move. We wanted to get on with making a difference.

Today, with the internet, management and business software resources, and social media, it is a new ballgame. These communication, organizational, and management tools have streamlined many of the functions necessary to effectively run a CBO. From public relations to budgeting, to development, to managing mailing and email lists of donors, to design, printing, and mailing fundraising materials, to advertising events, all have become much more accessible and manageable because of these tools. As a result, the distance between passion for a cause and having a direct, tangible, community impact has narrowed appreciably. The barriers between a vision and its transformation into action and impact have never been lower. Today if you have a cause you believe in or an issue you want to impact, simply set up a website and you are in business. And you go from there. That's exciting because you never know where that simple, first step might take you.

In short, this is on us as Old White Dudes. Silence is no longer an option and talk is cheap. Why not turn the advantages that result from your White privilege into actions and a force for good? Whatever the issue, there is a world of opportunity and possibilities available to make a difference. The question is whether you want to make the commitment to do something—anything, big or small—to make a difference or to change a life.

Jim Morrissey, a friend from my graduate school days at Ohio University has coached a youth basketball team in Chicago for almost twenty years. Essentially, he is the only White person involved in the league. In describing his experience, he said, "It's not like you are going to a meeting of the local garden or investment club. You can't go through the motions. You have to leave your White privilege at the door because none of these kids or their family members care about that. All they care about is whether you are a good person who is honest and going to work hard to be a good coach. Your stuff better be solid, or they will see right through you."

He contrasts that with being in groups of all White people where you "chitchat incessantly about the same stuff with the same people with the same attitudes, backgrounds and beliefs." He talks about the importance of putting yourself in situations where you are the minority in a different culture and environment. It's not easy. It is extremely challenging, daunting, and in fact, can be a bit scary. There's uncertainty. It requires work to successfully navigate those differences and challenges. But the result is new experiences, new perspectives, and ultimately meaningful growth and increased understanding and empathy regarding the lives of people who do not look like us. And tremendous potential rewards! You might have an opportunity to change a life and make a real difference.

And please don't be overwhelmed that you are not doing enough. Don't let that paralyze you. *Just do something!* What you will likely find is that, in doing so, you will meet other people who are also committed to doing something to advance issues relating to social justice and human dignity. You might also find that the more you become involved in a hands-on fashion, the more involved you may want to become. If you give it a chance, it can be gratifying, nourishing, and uplifting work.

While I hope these suggestions have been helpful, Michael Eric Dyson offers additional suggestions for specific actions to take in the fight against racism. In his wonderful book, *Tears We Cannot Stop*, he describes forms of reparations to Black Americans, which "descendants of enslaved Africans should receive from the society that exploited them some form of compensation." (Dyson 2017, 2021, 198)

This is a contentious issue. Many people find it difficult to embrace reparations to Black Americans who were not enslaved, as the burden for reparations might fall on people who played no part in slavery. Why should living descendants of slaves be provided anything? We now have civil rights laws in place. The social and cultural playing field has been evened out. These days, we all have the same rights and opportunities.

Dyson responds. "Surely you can see the justice of making reparation, even if you can't make it happen politically. Please don't say that your ancestors didn't own slaves. Your white privilege has not been hampered by that fact. Black sweat built the country you now reside in, and you continue to enjoy the fruits of that labor." (Dyson 2017, 2021, 198)

He provides specifics of reparation work. For example, hire Black folk at your company and pay them slightly better than you would ordinarily pay them. Or pay the Black person who cuts your lawn double the going rate. Or identify a deserving Black student and provide scholarship help or send a child whose family can't afford it to summer camp. He also suggests you can influence your civic organization or church to commit a tenth of its resources to educating Black youth. He terms these actions *secular tithe.* Dyson's examples are perfectly reasonable and achievable. In other words, you don't have to be Bill Gates to make a big difference.

He adds other suggestions, beginning with the importance of educating yourself about Black life and culture. He writes, "Racial literacy is as necessary as it is undervalued." (Dyson 2017, 2021, 199) He then provides an excellent, broad, and comprehensive list of books and resources to better understand the history and realities of being Black in America. From James Baldwin to Toni Morrison, from DuBois to Obama, from Malcom X to Henry Louis Gates, and from Ralph Ellison to Zora Neale Hurston. There is plenty of reading to keep you busy. I know it will keep me busy for a long time.

Once you do your research and become more educated about Black culture and history, he urges you to school your friends and family about that culture and history as well as our White privilege. He writes, "[T]here is only so much I can say to white folk, only so much they can hear from me or anyone who isn't white. They may not be as defensive with you, so you must be an ambassador of truth to your own tribes." (Dyson 2017, 2021, 203)

Dyson doesn't stop there. He encourages White folk to participate in protests, rallies, and community meetings. I attended several rallies and marches in Lancaster after the George Floyd murder where it got intense. But my general impression was that there were a lot of White people marching. Dyson says that it makes a huge difference when Whites attend these rallies and marches. He explained, "When we gather to express grief, outrage and dissent, your presence sends the signal that this is not 'just a black thing.' It is, instead, an American thing. Your white bodies don't just disintegrate the images that communicate social concern. Your presence also puts your bodies and reputations on the line by identifying you with folk you are not supposed to have much in common with. Your presence adds greater moral weight to the gathering. It shouldn't have to be that way, but for now, it is." (Dyson 2017, 2021, 205)

So, dust off your marching shoes.

He also encourages us to actively seek out Black people as real friends, as opposed to simply tokens. Again, his explanation for why that is so important makes complete sense. "Every open-minded white person should set out immediately to find and make friends with black folk who share their interests. It's not as hard as it seems. Black folk come in every variety of belief, ideology, and politics, just as any other American does, and the vast majority of us are morally upright." (Dyson 2017, 2021, 207)

We can all use new friends. Why shouldn't some of them be POC?

He also stresses the importance of us OWDs speaking up against racial injustice. He quotes Martin Luther King, Jr., who said that we would have to repent not only for the "evil words and deeds of the bad people, but for the appalling silence of the good people." Dyson follows with, "We need to hear your voices ring out against our suffering loud and clear." (P 207)

If we believe we are "good people" then why do we remain silent?

My older brother Tom is a contractor in Lynchburg, VA. His real passion, however, is Habitat for Humanity. He has built a network of volunteers throughout the country who twice a year converge on a city or town to work with the local Habitat affiliate to engage in a Blitz Build. These are marvelous, inspiring events. Anywhere from fifty to 100 out-of-towners show up to a build site where the foundations for two or three houses have been laid. Over the course of the weekend, the "Habitat Crazies" work together to build the rest of the house. It is tremendously gratifying when you walk onto the site with nothing but a foundation and walk away two days later with two or three houses built. He also travels around the country as a motivational speaker for the Habitat cause. He's so committed and effective as an advocate and organizer of these events that he received the Habitat for Humanity National Volunteer of the Year award in 2002. Clearly, our parents were pretty good teachers regarding the importance of community service.

Tom often talks about how people are hungry to feel that feeling of helping to move the world forward. In his presentation, titled "Aspire to Inspire Before you Expire," he talks about how the world can be changed by joining our hearts and hands and he challenges others to "let your heart tell your hands what to do." After reading an early draft of this manuscript, he wrote to me, "All that is necessary is to make the first step an easy one. Once they get a taste of it and realize they can change the world, they are never the same and there is no stopping them." He continued, "Not only do Old White Dudes need to join hands with people of color, but OWDs need to bring more OWDs along with them. It's always better to dance with a partner."

I suppose it is fitting to bring this section to a close with a passage from Martin Luther King. It is the last paragraph from his masterful work, *Where Do We Go from Here: Chaos or Community.* "We are now faced with the fact that tomorrow is today. We are confronted with the fierce urgency of *now*. In this unfolding conundrum of life and history there is such a thing as being too late. Procrastination is still the thief of time. Life often leaves us standing bare, naked and dejected with a lost opportunity. The 'tide in the affairs of men' does not remain at the flood; it ebbs. We may cry out desperately for time to pause in her passage, but time is deaf to every plea and rushes on. Over the bleached bones and jumbled residues of numerous civilizations are written the pathetic words: 'Too late.' There is an invisible book of life that faithfully records our vigilance or our neglect. 'The moving finger writes, and having writ, moves on . . .' We still have a choice today: nonviolent coexistence or violent coannihilation. This may well be mankind's last chance to choose between chaos and community." (King 1968, 202)

King wrote those words in 1967. They remain relevant today.

I do believe we White folks can meet this challenge. I do believe in people's better angels. And I do believe that people are in fact, hungry to make a difference. But this can't wait. It is time to act.

For as long as I can remember, at least twice a week, my mother volunteered at a soup kitchen that served the poor in a mostly Black and Hispanic neighborhood in Paterson, New Jersey. She served meals and did whatever was needed, all the while offering smiles and words of encouragement to anyone who entered the building. She was interested in their stories and asked them about their lives. She treated them with love and compassion. She often took us with her. It was clear that she was beloved by the staff as well as those receiving the meals. She did this until her late seventies. One of my most vivid memories of my mother was when she, a two-time cancer survivor and in failing health, was still arranging for her friends to pick her up for the ride into the city. She'd shuffle out our front door, pulling her oxygen tank behind her to the waiting car. She was a tiny, wisp of a woman, but she was a force of nature, exuding power, purpose, and commitment to make a difference. She didn't talk much about it; her actions spoke volumes.

At the end of the day, if my mother can drag her oxygen tank out our front door down to the soup kitchen at age seventy-five and in failing health, surely we all can do *something*.

It's time we get on it!

# NARRATED BIBLIOGRAPHY

*"The only thing necessary for the triumph of evil is for good men to do nothing."*

—Edmund Burke

As referenced in Chapter Six, doing the work of reading, watching, asking questions, and listening to increase our understanding of the history of systemic racism, is a critical step in becoming a positive force for social justice and equity. And in Chapters Seven through Ten, I offered a few of the most influential books I've read on that history. But these books represent a small sample of the resources I have found educational and inspiring. Following are additional resources, in no particular order. My hope is that my brief descriptions of the information contained within will spur you to further explore them as you engage in your own social justice work.

As in Chapter Six, we will begin with James Baldwin. Simply put, James Baldwin was one of the most powerful and compelling writers to ever walk the face of the earth. My guess is that most White folks have not read much Baldwin. He wasn't included in the curriculum of my high school and college or, if so, only mentioned in passing. That is educational malpractice on two levels. First, his perspective and thoughts on the Black experience in America are as provocative as it gets.

Second, as a writer, I reveled in the way he used language and words as *ammunition* in the moral debate regarding civil rights. It was novelist and playwright Edward Bulwer-Lytton who, in 1839, wrote "the pen is mightier than the sword." If there has ever been a writer whose use of language personifies that adage, it's Baldwin. Any time spent reading James Baldwin is time well spent. But be prepared. He will twist your mind in ways you never imagined. For starters, read his essay "My Dungeon Shook: Letter to My Nephew on the One Hundredth Anniversary of the Emancipation." I'd also highly encourage reading the *The Fire Next Time*, particularly the last quarter of the book. This is some of the most powerful and provocative writing on race in America ever put to the page. If you are more of a visual learner, I'd recommend pulling up "James Baldwin and William F. Buckley 1965 debate on Race in America" on You Tube. These resources will give you a taste of James Baldwin. But be forewarned, you will be challenged in ways you have never been challenged before.

In 1967, Dr. Martin Luther King, Jr. isolated himself in a rented house in Jamaica with no telephone, and wrote *Where Do We Go from Here: Community or Chaos?* It was to be his final manuscript before he was assassinated. During the process of reading this work, I found myself going back to this manuscript and adding many of his passages to support and bolster arguments or points I was making. His work was so expansive, thoughtful, and descriptive of the challenges, issues, and history relating to civil and human rights, that it got to a point where I decided that rather than quoting him extensively throughout my manuscript, I should simply recommend the entire book as a must read. And in the tradition of Frederick Douglass and James Baldwin, his ability to turn a phrase and use words as precision instruments to drive home a point or narrative is not only extraordinary, but inspiring

Before moving on from Dr. King, I would be remiss to not mention some of his signature speeches and essays, including his "I Have a Dream" speech, (Washington D.C. August 28, 1963), in which he called for an end to racism before a crowd of 250,000, "Beyond Vietnam – A Time to Break the Silence" (Riverside Church, NYC. April 4, 1967), in which he condemned the war, even though the public still supported it, and his final speech, delivered in Memphis on April 3, 1968, titled, "I've Been to the Mountaintop." You can read these, but better yet, watch them on YouTube.

Finally, I encourage you to read King's "Letter from Birmingham

Jail." This is one of the most thoughtful, compelling, and powerful pieces in the history of American literature. King was arrested in Birmingham and sent to jail for protesting segregation. His letter, written from jail, was in response to an open letter from eight White clergymen that appeared in the *Birmingham News* on April 13, 1963. The clergymen criticized King and his fellow activists as being "outsiders coming in". To whet your appetite, here's a particularly powerful passage from his letter:

"I am cognizant of the interrelatedness of all communities and states. I cannot sit idly by in Atlanta and not be concerned about what happens in Birmingham. Injustice anywhere is a threat to justice everywhere. We are caught in an inescapable network of mutuality, tied in a single garment of destiny. Whatever affects one directly affects all indirectly. Never again can we afford to live with the narrow, provincial 'outside agitator' idea. Anyone who lives inside the United States can never be considered an outsider."

And that is simply a snippet of the brilliance of the Reverend Dr. Martin Luther King, Jr.

Another book that has influenced my thinking has been *How to be an Anti-Racist* by Ibram X. Kendi. Again, different people may interpret Kendi's ideas and writings in different ways. What I offer here is my interpretation. In a nutshell, the thread that runs through this book is the idea that it is not enough to not be racist in your attitudes, beliefs, and actions, but that you must be actively *antiracist* as it applies to those beliefs and actions.

This book was particularly instructive and inspiring in that he makes the important distinction between talking about racism or expressing support for social justice and actively engaging in behaviors to address injustice and discrimination. It relates directly, at least in my mind, to the notion of an individual or organization having to take that first step in making a conscious, directed decision to begin to do something concrete on behalf of social justice.

While we are on Kendi, his *Stamped from the Beginning: The Definitive History of Racist Ideas in America* is another great resource.

The winner of many book awards, including the National Book Award for Nonfiction, it is an expansive, intellectual look at the history of prejudice and racism in America. This is an important, foundational book regarding the Black experience in America.

"The 1619 Project: A New Origin Story" is an ongoing project from *The New York Times* Magazine that began in August 2019, the four hundredth anniversary of the first enslaved Blacks reaching our shores. It is led by Pulitzer Prize-winning journalist Nikole Hannah-Jones. It has gotten a lot of attention and generated a lot of controversy. As the title suggests, at its core this is an origin story. She writes:

"Origin stories function, to a degree, as myths designed to create a shared sense of history and purpose. Nations simplify these narratives in order to unify and glorify, and those origin stories serve to illuminate how a society wants to see itself—and how it doesn't. The origin story of the United States that we tell ourselves through textbooks and films, monuments and museums, public speeches and public histories, the one that most defines our national identity, portrays an intrepid freedom loving people who rebelled against an oppressive monarchy, won their independence, tamed the West, advanced an exceptional nation based on the radical ideals of self-governance and equality, and heroically fought a civil war to end slavery and preserve that nation. This mythology has positioned almost exclusively white Americans as the architects and champions of democracy. And because of this, some have believed that white people should disproportionately reap the benefits of this democracy." (Hannah-Jones 2021, 452)

Hannah-Jones explains that the point of the 1619 Project is to show that America's origin story is neither accurate nor complete unless we recognize the essential role that Black Americans have played in that story.

I've mentioned how it has been White men who have written our collective history which, in large part, has resulted in the whitewashing of the role Black Americans, slavery, and Jim Crow have played in that history. That being the case, it is no surprise that such whitewashing has become a part of what our schools teach regarding this subject. In his provocative and beautifully written work, titled, *How the Word is Passed: A Reckoning with the History of Slavery Across America*, Clint Smith, who I am proud to say is a graduate of my alma mater, Davidson College, highlights how this alternative history goes beyond what is taught in our schools. Smith has toured and studied many monuments, landmarks, and resource centers throughout the US that purport to tell the stories and history of slavery and its ongoing impact on American society. Smith traveled to several historical sites that portray themselves as educational and historical resources. From Thomas Jefferson's Monticello to Angola, a former plantation turned maximum security prison in Louisiana, to Blandford Cemetery, a gravesite in Virginia for thousands of Confederate soldiers, Smith took tours, listened to the various tour guides, and researched and reviewed the various historical information produced by them. What he found was that there is a wide discrepancy among these sites as it pertains to just how accurate and honest a portrayal they present regarding the legacy of slavery. Some of them make an honest effort at portraying that legacy, warts and all, while others not so much. As the title suggests, this book is about how we tell our history or how the word is passed. I suppose this is not terribly surprising as if you own the historical site or are the managers of such sites, you get to write the narratives around the role and stories of slavery. Smith looks under the veil that is presented by these sites and monuments to reveal that when it comes to telling our collective stories or history around racism and slavery, it's important to *trust but verify.* Like the victors being able to write the history, so to do the owners of such sites get to write the historical narratives associated with them. This is an excellent read.

And while we are on books written by Davidson College alums, there is *The Movement Made Us: A Father, A Son, and the Legacy of a Freedom Ride* by David Dennis, Jr., in collaboration with his father, David Dennis, Sr. This book is for those who are interested in getting a sense of what it was like to be a part of the civil rights movement of the 1960's. It is a brilliant, searing behind the scenes look at those who so tirelessly and courageously worked and fought for civil rights. It is also a father-son story of heartache, pain, and ultimately reconciliation and love. David's father was a major architect and organizer of the movement, from the freedom bus rides to voter registration, working through organizations such as the NAACP, CORE and SNCC, primarily in Mississippi and Louisiana. In short, David Dennis, Sr. was right in the middle of all of it. Dennis, Jr., through a series of interviews, sets up a framework for his father to, for the first time, write of his experiences as a civil rights organizer. This gives you an unsettling glimpse of the terrors of being Black in America during those tumultuous times. His stories highlight not only his unyielding conviction and incredible courage in facing down discrimination, hate, and violence but also the hundreds of other freedom fighters who literally put their lives on the line daily in the struggle for social justice and human dignity. This was another eye-opening book in that as much as you try to imagine the depth of the hatred and violence towards Black Americans, the stories are simply gut wrenching. As Dennis, Jr. writes "the cruelty is relentless." (P. 252)

I have quoted Michael Eric Dyson's work throughout this text, particularly *Tears We Cannot Stop: A Sermon to White America*. This is for good reason as Dyson is one of America's premier public intellectuals and author of seven *New York Times* best sellers. He is also a preacher and uses a format that preachers and ministers, at least good ones, use well; the sermon. This book is wildly informative as he provides many illuminating observations and provocative narratives, including what is the most graphic description of what it must feel like to be stopped by the police. His chapter titled "Copotopia" is brilliant. If you read nothing else in his book, read this chapter. He writes of several personal and disturbing (but hardly surprising) encounters with the police, which can happen at any moment in any place and for any, or no, reason at all. As he says, "It is our routine, our daily ritual of survival." (171)

He continues. "You cannot know the terror that black folk feel when a cop car makes its approach and the history of racism and violence comes crashing down on us. The police car is a mobile plantation, and the siren is the sound of dogs hunting us down in the dark woods.

"My friends, please don't pretend you can't understand how we feel this way. And if you claim that slavery and Jim Crow and the sixties are ancient history, you know your words are lies before they leave your lips. How could that history be erased so quickly?" (181, 182)

Dyson then brings this very powerful chapter to a close with this thought. "Beloved, you must not be defensive when you hear our hurt. We who proclaim the terror of cops do not hate all cops. We hate what cops have been made to be. We hate that cops don't treat us the way they treat you . . . We do not hate you, white America. We hate that you terrorize us and then lie about it and then make us feel crazy for having to explain to you how crazy it makes us feel. We cannot hate you, not really, not most of us; that is our gift to you. We cannot halt you; that is our curse." (191, 193)

Dyson serves up some powerful, provocative stuff.

That noted, Dyson goes on to explain that the vast majority of Black Americans still believe in the promise of the country. Dyson turns to MLK, who declared that White America had to do Blacks right, yet he spoke for most of us when he said, "We ain't going nowhere." (P. 115) After all the reading, research, videos, and discussions I've accessed in my work to educate myself on the Black experience in America, what may be most amazing and inspiring is how, after all the history of abuse and hate, Black Americans continue to love and sacrifice for our nation, including for us White Americans. When you consider the enormity of their struggle, you can't help but to shake your head in amazement and wonder at the grace, forgiveness, patience, and love that requires.

Another informative book is *Four Hundred Souls: A Community History of African-America, 1619-2019*, edited by Ibram X. Kendi and Keisha N. Blain. I'll quote the description that appears on the book jacket. The editors have "assembled ninety brilliant writers, each of whom takes on a brief period of that 400-hundred-year span (the year that the first Blacks arrived on our shores (1619) to the present). The writers explore their periods through a variety of techniques; historical essays, short stories, personal vignettes, and fiery polemics."

Typically, there are a few names and incidents with which most Americans are familiar. Martin Luther King, Jr., Rosa Parks, and John Lewis, and events like the Civil Rights marches of the 1960's are referenced and studied. But not much more of Black American history is taught.

What is so illuminating about this work is that for all the people, events, and places relating to civil rights and Black history that whites are somewhat familiar with, there are literally thousands of people and events we've never heard of and know nothing about. The discriminatory and criminal acts, policies, and stories are endless. And the incredibly heroic stories of individuals making a stand for civil rights are simply inspiring. There are so many horrific stories of crimes against Black people as well as compelling and inspiring stories of the bravery and perseverance of people who, in far too many cases, gave their lives for the cause of social justice. Most of them, however, have been whitewashed from US history. Kendi and Blain provide a tremendous service in uncovering and illuminating the people and events that should be a part our collective historical knowledge base.

Speaking of a historical figure who White America has largely ignored, Ida B. Wells-Barnett was as courageous a fighter for truth and social justice as we've ever seen. Born into slavery during the Civil War in Mississippi, she rose to become one of the most important journalists and activists in American history. While early in life she worked as a teacher and educator, her greatest impact resulted from her considerable skills as a journalist fighting sexism, racism, and violence. Her investigations and writings on lynching in America shed light on the widespread nature of White mob violence. She traveled internationally to draw attention to these issues. She also confronted White women in the suffrage movement who ignored Black women. In reading her autobiography, titled *Crusade for Justice,* I was continually amazed at the risks she took in her efforts to shed light on the events around her. She was absolutely fearless and a true American hero. Sadly, she has, for the most part, been left out of the historical accounting of our nation's history.

Do you ever wonder what the conversation or *the talk* that Black parents give their children about how to remain safe in the streets might sound like? *In Between the World and Me*, by Ta-Nehisi Coates provides a compelling glimpse. The book takes the form of a letter from Coates to his adolescent son. The essential question he explores is what it is like, as noted on the book jacket, "to inhabit a Black body and how to find a way to live within it." It's a powerful, provocative read.

From Coates we will move to an example of the types of things you run across as you delve deeper into the history of race in America. I had never given much consideration to the role religion, and particular, white evangelicals, have played in that history. *White Evangelical Racism: The Politics of Morality in America* by Anthea Butler, assistant professor of religion at the University of Pennsylvania and a former evangelical herself, provided some eye-opening revelations. Butler explores how, despite their presumed morality, White evangelicals have used that claim of morality to hide the fact that racism is a foundational principle of their core beliefs and political activism. While she acknowledges that many evangelicals were abolitionists, supported the poor and did mission work, "many also supported slavery, split churches, believed African Americans were inferior to Whites, supported Jim Crow, and avidly opposed civil rights, busing, and interracial marriage. Many harassed gays, called AIDS a curse from God, and vilified Muslims after 9/11. So, when evangelical writers claim that they do not understand the overwhelming nature of evangelical support for right wing and downright scurrilous Republican candidates and policies, they fail to reckon with evangelical history." (P. 9) If you are interested in a clear-eyed, unvarnished look at that history, this is a great place to start.

Another excellent resource is a TEDX speech by Nita Mosby Tyler, titled "What if White People Led the Charge to End Racism?" Her fundamental point is that justice requires accomplices. She notes that it takes love and courage for Whites to stand with the oppressed and that where there is no justice, "you must create it and build it." She goes on the make the point that if it's the same people who always speak out, meaningful change never occurs. As with trying to build anything, whether a business, non-profit organization, house, or social justice movement, you do it brick by brick or, in this case, person by person.

We need new voices, including yours. The time is ripe with opportunity to make a difference. When you raise your voice, it will inspire and encourage others to do the same. Tyler encourages us to stand up for what is right even when we feel out of place because "justice counts on all of us" and that "change is collective work."

The question is whether we will hear your voice. As Otis S. Johnson, educator, civic leader and former mayor of Savannah, Georgia wrote, "If you believe in a cause, be willing to stand up for that cause with a million people, or by yourself."

In the introduction to *Letters to My White Male Friends*, Dax-Devlon Ross writes this to his intended audience of White people, "You and I both know that you hold immense power, wealth, and status in our society. That power strikes fear and invokes intimidation. It instills a sense of incontestable authority and certainty. No one challenges you to push beyond your comfort zones. In short, when it comes to conversations about race, white men are typically coddled and appeased." (8)

By now, you are very familiar with what Ross is referring to—White fragility. From Kendi to DiAngelo, Dyson to Baldwin and many others, they all mention it in some form or another as it is arguably the biggest roadblock to racial reconciliation. While Ross is very direct in his message to Whites, he expresses it in a way that seems more accessible. He strikes a balance between making you uncomfortable but at the same time providing some space and grace for you to contemplate and grow. With Ross you are comfortable feeling uncomfortable.

It's a very accessible read, but at the same time challenges your conceptions and notions around issues of how we, as Whites, distance ourselves from the ugliest, most vile aspects and behaviors of racism, thus allowing us to "comfortably tell ourselves that we're not racist since we're not or would never do *that*. That disgust with and desire to distance ourselves from racism's ugliest expressions blocks us from probing beneath the surface." (147) Ross does a good job in nudging us to probe beneath the surface.

These books are all very powerful and at times, difficult to work through because they challenge many of our preconceptions and behaviors. As a change of pace, here are a few books that are more about providing a historical account of Black history. They are a bit lighter, but every bit as fascinating and informative.

While we need to hear historical accounts because they are factual, fictional works by Black novelists are important as well. Historical accounts and novels provide exposure to what the Black experience might have looked and felt like. There is a difference between talking about and acknowledging the realities of slavery in a general sense. But seeing an image or photo or reading a novelist's vivid description of a lynching or a beating or an account of Black folk being denied the right to vote is different. The historian or novelist brings those scenes vividly to life. As uncomfortable as that might be for us OWDs or our children or grandchildren, we need to see these images and hear the stories behind them. If we do not see and feel this history and hear these stories, we will never develop any sense of empathy for the plight of Black Americans. Our ability as White Americans to feel that empathy is a critical ingredient for racial healing.

If you are not familiar with Frederick Douglass, you are missing one of the most powerful, inspiring stories in American history. He was simply a giant of a man. Historian David Blight brings him to life in *Frederick Douglass: Prophet of Freedom*.

To give you a sense of Douglass's status and influence, I'll quote from the book jacket. "Frederick Douglass was the most important African American of the nineteenth century and one of the most significant writers and orators in American history. Douglass was born a slave and escaped at the age of twenty. . . . Over his lifetime, he wrote three versions of his autobiography, all of which are classics of the slave narrative and of American memoir. The former slave met with Lincoln in the White House and rejoiced in the victory of emancipation. He saw the promise of Reconstruction dashed by the resistance of former slaveholders and their allies and fought this betrayal as ferociously as he had fought slavery itself. As a lecturer he likely reached more listeners than any American of his century."

While reading this book, I often shook my head in disbelief, inspired by the courage, wisdom, vision, persistence, and impact of this man.

And while we are on Frederick Douglass, I'd also highly recommend reading his "The Hypocrisy of American Slavery", which he delivered on July 5, 1852. It will give you a better understanding of why Black Americans aren't all that excited to celebrate July 4, 1776, as marking our nation's birth of freedom.

"This Fourth of July is yours, not mine. You may rejoice, I must mourn . . . Do you mean, citizens, to mock me, by asking me to speak to-day?" he wrote. Douglass was simply reminding America that when the Declaration of Independence was signed, most Blacks were still slaves. In fact, it was more likely that the British would offer Blacks freedom than the colonists. Therefore, many Black Americans consider Juneteenth (June 19) as their Independence Day. Given the history, why wouldn't they?

On January 1, 1863, Abraham Lincoln signed the Emancipation Proclamation, freeing the slaves. Somehow, word of that development did not reach Texas until June 19, 1865, when Union soldiers arrived in Galveston with the news. There are several theories why word was late in arriving, from a messenger on the way to delivering the news being murdered to slaveholders deliberately withholding the information. Regardless, enslaved people in Texas continued living in bondage for almost two and a half years despite being legally free. Given that bit of history, it is not surprising that Black Americans would celebrate Juneteenth as the date of their true freedom. As the history behind what Juneteenth really means has become more widely known, an increasing number of people have supported the drive to establish it as a national holiday. That drive became a reality in 2021, when President Joe Biden signed a declaration designating Juneteenth as a federal holiday. We'll take that as progress.

*The Warmth of Other Suns: The Epic Story of America's Great Migration* by Isabel Wilkerson is a work of narrative nonfiction. It is beautifully written and absolutely spellbinding. Wilkerson chronicles the decades long migration of almost six million Black Americans who fled the South from 1915-1970 for Northern and Western cities in search of a better life. It reads like a novel as she personalizes the full spectrum of stories, from the triumphs to the indignities. Even though it is one of the most significant historical events in American history, my guess is that it is hardly mentioned in history classes. It's time to familiarize yourself with an event that literally changed the face and character of America.

*Warmth of Other Suns* tells the stories of three Black Americans who migrated out of the Jim Crow South to Chicago, New York, and Los Angeles. She traces their respective journeys from their desperate situations in the South to their escapes and chronicles their lives in their new cities. She interviewed more than a thousand individuals, so the accounts and stories are personal. She weaves those personal stories into a broader historical treatment of the Great Migration and shows how each of these individuals were impacted along the way. Her ability to make this a personal, intimate account of their lives brings everything to life. You can visualize their worlds and feel their frustrations, fears, and doubts.

These are real stories of real people. And if you think that all the discrimination, brutalization, and cruel treatment of those who migrated from the Jim Crow South ended when they arrived in the North, you are sadly mistaken. This book will give you a better understanding of that bitter reality.

As for works of fiction regarding the Black experience there is no shortage of great Black novelists. From Toni Morrison to Langston Hughes, from Ralph Ellison to Maya Angelou, there are plenty to choose from.

These and other writers bring the harsh realities of the Black experience to life. They make it real. In some ways, their storytelling is as close as us OWDs will get to, if not fully understanding, at least providing a greater understanding of those realities. Again, while reading these accounts will not equate to living their reality, they help you visualize and imagine it and, on some level, feel it.

For another resource that brings these realities to life is *The Personal Librarian* by Marie Benedict and Victoria Christopher Murray. It is a historical fiction account of the life of Belle de Costa Greene, who was hired by J.P. Morgan to curate his personal collection of ancient manuscripts and artwork for his library. Belle became a well-known, highly respected fixture of New York society and the world of global fine art. She was considered one of, if not the most, successful female businesspeople of her time (early to mid- 1900's). But Belle had a secret that she had to protect at all costs. She was the daughter of Richard Greener, the first Black graduate of Harvard University and an active civil rights advocate. As prefaced on the book jacket, this is "the story of an extraordinary woman, famous for her intellect, style, and wit, and shares the length she must go to—for the protection of her family and her legacy—to preserve her carefully crafted white identity in the racist world in which she lives." This is a fascinating read.

This brings us to another wonderful novel by Jodi Picoult, a white woman. *Small Great Things* is the story of a Black labor and delivery nurse (Ruth Jefferson) who, after performing routine checkup on a newborn was later told that she was no longer allowed to care for that child. The child's parents were White supremacists and did not want their child touched by a Black woman. The next day the child goes into cardiac distress while Ruth is alone with the child. The plot centers on what she does in that moment of crisis and the resulting fallout. The story is compelling and wonderfully written. But what stuck out most in my mind was something she wrote in the "Author's Notes" at the end of the book.

"When I was researching this book, I asked white mothers how often they talked about racism with their children. Some said occasionally; some admitted they never discussed it. When I asked the same question of Black mothers, they all said, *Every day.*" (463)

This is another example of how us OWDs might have *some* appreciation for the everyday struggles of POC in this White dominated culture of ours, but we have absolutely no understanding of the *magnitude* of the struggle to merely survive, let alone thrive, in America. In some ways, it's like Black Americans are always "behind enemy lines" in White America.

I'd also be remiss if I didn't encourage you to read some Colson Whitehead. I'm not going to get into specifics, other than to say this. He is the only writer ever to receive a Pulitzer Prize for two consecutive novels, *The Underground Railroad* and *The Nickle Boys*. Both are powerful narratives of the Black American experience. What can I possibly say about them other than, "Just read 'em!

If you want to take your research to the next level, check out this excellent ten-part series produced by Dartmouth College, "*The Historical Philosophy of W.E.B. DuBois*". DuBois was an American sociologist, intellectual, civil rights advocate, author, writer, and editor. He was the first Black American to earn a PhD from Harvard. And the modern day intellectual, writer, author and civil rights advocate conducting this lecture series is Cornel West. Not to make light of the gravity and substance of the material West covers, but this is must-see TV! West weaves a diverse array of references, resources, and examples to highlight DuBois's work. And he does it without notes. His style is engaging and entertaining. Not only is this lecture series extremely educational, it is also a joy to watch.

The purpose of Chapter Six and this narrated bibliography was to provide potential resources for you to access as you begin to do the necessary research and work of increasing your knowledge base around issues of justice and race. That said, the items mentioned only scratch the surface of what is available for consumption and consideration. It is my hope that the list, as well as my short summaries and reflections, will inspire you to dig a little deeper in your research, to provide a bit of history and perspective as you begin your own journey to become a more effective racial justice advocate and ally.

As mentioned, while initial steps in your journey include making the decision to commit to action and listening to POC and their stories with humility and an open mind, they are preludes to the next critical step. Specifically, it is committing to do the work—the reading, researching and thoughtful contemplation required to become a more informed and committed advocate for social justice and equity.

## MY RECIPE FOR GUMBO FOR JUSTICE

*"One of the things that's beautiful about New Orleans is how culturally rich we are and how well we have worked together. People call us a gumbo. It's really important that we get focused on the very simple notion that diversity is a strength. It's not a weakness."*

—Mitch Landrieu, former mayor of New Orleans

What does gumbo have to do with social justice? As it turns out, a lot. There are a series of decisions, commitments, and steps required to make a good, thick, tasty pot of gumbo. Similarly, there are a series of decisions, commitments, and steps to becoming a force against racism.

A quick Google search reveals at least 317 gumbo recipes. Similarly, there are many ways to draw attention to and promote better understanding of issues relating to justice, equity, and diversity. This is my personal recipe for becoming a positive force in the struggle for social justice and human dignity. It is offered in the hope that you might consider not only my ingredients and process, but that you might even consider *tasting* it. And, if you like it, perhaps you will treat yourself to a full helping.

First, a note. I had never heard of Eddie Francis and his "Theory of Gumbo" until I finished writing my own. When someone pointed out that he had also used this metaphor to highlight diversity, I was concerned that my recipe might be considered plagiarism. While there are a few themes that may be similar, Francis's work is geared more specifically to promoting diversity in Greek life on college campuses (https://www.watchtheyard.com/chapter-leadership/eddie-francis-gumbo-theory/). Another difference is that Francis writes that the key to a good gumbo is the roux. Clearly, he's a much better and more knowledgeable cook than I. He's also a native of New Orleans, which might explain why. Regardless, I concocted my Theory of Gumbo long before I knew of his. Still, I felt responsible to cite his work even though our respective theories differ enough to allow me to offer mine for consideration. Writers and theorists regularly build upon existing theories, philosophies, and lines of thought. That's how thinking and knowledge evolves. Not to mention it's how we pass down and improve recipes from generation to generation.

Here is my Recipe for Gumbo for Justice.

DECISION TO MAKE THE GUMBO: The first step in making gumbo is to decide to make the gumbo! It is not an easy dish to make. It takes time and effort. It's a big decision, particularly for anyone not an experienced or confident cook. Similarly, you must decide to do something (as opposed to simply talking about it) to be a part of the solution around issues of racism and diversity.

PREPARATION: While I didn't last more than a couple of weeks in the Boy Scouts (One camping trip with an outhouse as the only amenity cured me of that), I do remember the Boy Scout motto, "Be Prepared." That is great advice when it comes to making gumbo and great advice when trying to navigate issues relating to social justice. Thorough preparation is necessary to put you in a good position to make the gumbo. You must create a grocery list and shop to obtain all the ingredients and spices. Next is the prep work of washing the ingredients, slicing, and dicing them, and preparing the pots and pans. In short, you must do your homework by putting in the work in learning the recipe, identifying and procuring the ingredients, and properly preparing them.

Similarly, becoming a social justice ally requires reading and research. It's also about thoughtfully contemplating not only the history and current realities of racism, but also the role that you might be playing in perpetuating them.

As with any homework assignment, it also requires critical, thoughtful reflection and self-examination. Again, like a good gumbo, you've got to let that new knowledge and understanding marinate in your heart and mind. Given the subject matter, it's likely that if you engage in honest, critical, and thoughtful self-examination it will cause some discomfort. You will likely discover ways in which you have been contributing to maintaining systemic racism without even knowing it. It is messy and unsettling. But that's the point. If you don't face these issues and feel uncomfortable, the racial status quo in general and your role in maintaining that system will never change.

Doing the necessary homework not only illuminates, but it can also be tremendously gratifying. While I considered myself to be reasonably educated about this history and these issues, that education barely scratched the surface in terms of helping to better understand issues around racism and diversity. Like cooking a pot of gumbo, it takes work. But in doing that work, over time, you learn and improve. That makes the hard work worth it.

ADDING SPICES: We all love to eat a good, thick, tasty 'Nawlins gumbo. And washing it down with a few beers only makes it better. It's one of life's greatest pleasures. The secret to a great gumbo rests in the mixture and interplay between the various spices that are added and then simmered. The result is a full, complex, multi-layered texture that is rich and delicious. If you only use one or two spices, while it may taste good, it will be nowhere near as rich and dynamic in taste as gumbo made with many spices. The more spices the better.

It's the same with businesses, communities, and personal lives; the more diverse, the better. Acknowledging, embracing, and encouraging diversity only makes us stronger because we all— White, Black, Asian, Hispanic, LGBTQ+, and immigrants and refugees—possess and contribute unique talents and perspectives relating to the world around us. Or, if we want to keep the story in New Orleans, it's like a good jazz combo. If all the players in a jazz group, regardless of its size, possess the exact same style, sound, or approach to the music, the sound produced will not be nearly as dynamic, expansive, unique, and powerful as a group with musicians from various musical backgrounds and perspectives. The key to powerful, dynamic music, as with a tasty gumbo, rests in the mix or blend of the individual ingredients into the greater whole.

Take the Rolling Stones. While Keith Richards and Mick Jagger are the front men, many, including Richards himself, credit the late drummer Charlie Watts as the key driver of their unique sound. The greatest rock and roll band in history was powered for over fifty years by a jazz drummer. Watt's different approach to the music added a unique spice that made the Stones' sound so special.

As with most everything in this wide, wonderful world, the sum is greater than the whole of its parts. A diverse group, working together not only makes a project or an organization better, it also challenges us as individuals to learn and grow from the experience of working with people of different backgrounds. If you only interact or work with people exactly like yourself, your capacity and potential to learn and grow is limited.

There are also several key personal ingredients and spices that should be a part of the justice recipe, beginning with tolerance. You might also want to stir in a bit of vulnerability. A sense of humility and humbleness are critical ingredients as is an open and curious mind. A scoop of persistence and determination is also required as there will be setbacks, disappointments, and doubts along the way.

Finally, a big slab of patience is necessary as meaningful change takes time. There is no finish line in this work. In his illuminating book, *Letter to My White Male Friends,* Dax-Devlon Ross beautifully captures the notion of the path to racial justice being long and challenging:

"Feelings will be hurt. Mistakes will be made. Diversity efforts will fail. None of that is reason to turn away. We don't quit on relationships when they hit a snag or disappoint us. We dig in. We get creative. We have to see this endeavor as essential, not mandatory. As a prerequisite to our collective destiny, not a requirement to clear our conscious. As long as the Black-white wealth divide remains as wide as the day Martin Luther

King died, we have work to do. As long as race determines everything from education to health outcomes to longevity, we have work to do. As a corollary, find your beauty in the struggle. If you only see racial justice as an arduous task of unlearning and learning, then it will feel like work. When you are able to experience the benefits of social-justice labor— authentic, trust-based relationships across difference; an awareness of the absurdity of a caste system based on skin color – you will feel a sense of levity that isn't dependent on blindness." (P. 205)

Before moving on, I'd strongly suggest that you read that quote again. It's that important.

And now a word on moderation. I'd also suggest that in matters of social justice, you don't want to add too much patience to the recipe. Like how adding too much salt or pepper to a recipe might throw off the balanced taste you desire, being too patient runs against the important notion of having, in the words of Martin Luther King, Jr., the "urgency of now" driving change. In short, if not now, then when?

Finally, a major part of learning and growing as it applies to understanding racism and its impacts will involve reaching out to various people, in particular POC, to ask their thoughts, opinions, and advice. In the case of creating and implementing Songs For Justice, I had to reach out to various individuals of color, many of whom I had never met. It was important to approach these individuals and issues with humility and listen respectfully to what they had to say. Humility is critical because we, as Old White Dudes, are pretty clueless about many of these issues. The willingness to acknowledge that and say it out loud is an important spice.

LET IT SIMMER: Once you do the prep work, add spices into the pot, and get the temperature just right, you've got to give it time to simmer. You've got to let all those spices and ingredients mill about and bump into each other in the pot with flame underneath. The combination of time and heat allows those ingredients to interact with each other, to *bump into* each other to create flavorful synergies. While each spice has a unique flavor, tasting them separately is not to taste gumbo. It is their interaction with each other, their blending together that creates the unique taste and experience that is gumbo. But that takes time.

Similarly, it takes time to create a more diverse, just, and equitable society. Change of this magnitude and difficulty does not occur overnight. Regardless, we must throw ourselves into the arena to engage in the fight, using the resources and talents we each possess. To think that the work will not be hard or that change will occur overnight is not realistic. Gumbo must simmer to come to fruition.

While the work can become heated, controversial, and contentious at times, the fact is, we need to live with and spend time with each other. We need to integrate our lives where we actively seek out opportunities to interact and bump into each other to create personal and group synergies. While each personality (spice) has a unique taste of its own, each of us separately does not produce a diverse business, organization, neighborhood, or society. It is the interaction among each other, the simmering together that creates an interactive, collaborative, environment conducive to producing progress and change with the result being a more diverse and effective business, community, and culture.

TRUST THE PROCESS: As with any complex recipe that takes a while to cook, there is an element of faith, trust, and belief that, once the prep is complete, the spices added for a perfect mix, and the temperature setting or fire perfectly calibrated, the simmering process will take over from there. Once that equilibrium is established, you can take a break. Pour yourself a drink. Relax a bit. And trust that all your preparation and the process will, in the end, result in a wonderfully tasty gumbo.

It's the same with fostering diversity. After the decision to be a part of the solution and doing the research and work, after adding your unique spice to a broader group of spices and allowing all those spices to simmer into a diverse mixture, you must trust the process. You trust that the kindness, patience, compassion, love, and understanding of people will eventually win out. If we are to move forward together to become a more compassionate and diverse community and society, we must have faith that most people want to do the right thing. Even those who may not think in those terms at first, if provided time, space, and grace to contemplate, understand and grow, may eventually join the cause.

This doesn't mean however, that you turn your back on things. During this phase of cooking, you must keep an eye on the temperature or flame to make sure it's not burning too brightly or hot. Or maybe it's not quite simmering enough, and you need to add some heat. It's the same when addressing issues of justice. You must continue to monitor the shifting realities on the ground and when circumstances change or an unexpected event alters the dynamics, you must recognize it, adjust, and act accordingly. In other words, even when making progress on these issues, you must keep thinking about how you might be able to do more and do it better.

SHARING THE GUMBO: After all the prep work, the slicing and dicing, the mixing of spices, the simmering and trusting in the process, the result will be a wonderfully rich and tasty gumbo. So, what's next?

You *share* it! You spread it around. You take a bowl to your next-door neighbor. Or you get on the phone to some friends and inform them, "Hey, I just made a big 'ole pot of gumbo. And I got some beer. Wanna come over?" It's a gift of love that you share.

It's the same with issues of racism, justice, and equity. Once you accept responsibility to do something and engage in the necessary work, you share what you've learned, seen, and experienced by becoming a social justice advocate. *You spread the word!* And you spread the love because, ultimately, it's not about bitterness and hate. It's about love.

MAKE ADJUSTMENTS: This is the final step. As with any complex recipe, after it's completed and you've enjoyed the fruits of your labor, you assess the process and ingredients, and make adjustments to improve it for the next time. Like learning about issues of social justice and becoming an advocate, you must continue to expand your education and knowledge base. While we all would love for these issues to be solved, the fact is, they are not going away anytime soon. It's an ongoing process.

New issues may emerge, new events may impact perspectives and public policies, new research may influence and change attitudes. Similar to how recipes can be adjusted, updated, and reconfigured to improve the dish—maybe more shrimp or perhaps a pinch more cayenne pepper—so too as it applies to how we approach issues of diversity, justice and equity. It's a journey that requires ongoing thought and attention because the world is always in flux.

Now that we've fully experienced the gumbo, how about a side dish to compliment it? Chefs often research various recipes, take elements from several, and mix them up to create an original recipe. Similarly, I've taken several recurring concepts, themes, and thoughts from various sources on how to combat injustice and put them together to create a Social Justice Gumbo side dish. Given how often I came across these ideas and concepts, it seems to me they are solid, time-tested ingredients. My hope is that you at least *smell* it (give it some thought) and even better, *taste* it (decide to do something). Even if you don't particularly like gumbo, or only want a few bites, we do not want you to go away with an empty stomach. That's what side dishes are for, to offer a culinary alternative, or in this case, an alternative way of becoming a force for justice and human dignity.

## RECIPE FOR A SOCIAL JUSTICE SIDE DISH FOR OLD WHITE DUDES

Step 1. Stop talking! It's time for us Old White Dudes to simply listen for a while.

Step 2. Listening means we let POC tell their stories. As has been well established, the White establishment has controlled the levers of power throughout our nation's history, including in the media and writing the historical narrative of racism in the United States. It's time that we listen to POC tell their stories from their perspective. We should listen carefully, thoughtfully, with humility and an open mind.

Step 3. Any Questions? After listening to those stories, you will have an opportunity to ask questions, with the purpose of coming to a better understanding of issues and concerns. Don't be afraid to ask questions.

If your questions are honest, heartfelt, and posed with humility, grace, and an open mind, no one will begrudge you asking them.

Step 4. Place yourself in the position of a POC in America today. Or, stated differently, walk a mile in their shoes before passing judgement. This takes imagination and empathy. Those characteristics are critical to gain a better understanding of the realities of being Black in the United States.

Step 5. Thoughtfully consider everything you have heard and learned. Take your time. Think it through. If you must return to step three to ask additional questions or to do more research, do so. You want to consider all the angles and possibilities before making such an important decision.

Step 6. Decision time. Where do you stand on these issues? This is your choice and your choice alone. But whatever you decide, you must own it. That said, the fundamental issue remains, which side of social justice and history do you wish to be on?

Between these two recipes, my hope is that you find one you like. While I'm sure there are better recipes and I know full well there are better cooks, these are two recipes that taste right to me. I hope you find them equally as tasty and that you will enjoy a big, hearty serving of both.

# MUSIC FOR EVERYONE'S STATEMENT ON RACIAL JUSTICE

**M**FE believes that justice, equal opportunity, and Black Lives Matter. If the combination of the pandemic and the murders of George Floyd, Breonna Taylor, and Ahmaud Arbery have revealed anything, it is how inequitable, in virtually every sense, our society remains.

MFE believes that when we witness injustice and inequity we all have a responsibility and indeed, the right, to speak out forcefully, and when necessary, to march peacefully, but most importantly to commit to the hard work of bringing about necessary change. This is that time.

We will continue to do that hard work using the three pillars of our fundamental mission as our guide, to cultivate the power of music as an educational, community building, and public health tool in Lancaster County.

Meaningful change requires access to educational opportunity. MFE has invested heavily and been actively involved in enhancing music education opportunities for students throughout the county, most of whom are from communities of color. The lessons in cooperation, tolerance, empathy, personal responsibility, creativity, and communication, and listening skills that are learned through music participation are precisely the skills necessary to develop the empathy and understanding required to bridge cultural differences. It is in that way that music teaches the empathy and acceptance vital in creating a society of culturally literate, understanding, and tolerant people.

As the universal language, music unites us in unique and uplifting ways, which is why its power and potential to break down barriers, increase understanding, and build bridges makes it so effective as a community building tool. In these days of mistrust, unrest, and division, we need to utilize this powerful tool to rebuild and unite our communities.

Music also heals. Issues surrounding isolation, hopelessness, injustice, and inequality are excruciatingly difficult and painful. Music can soothe our souls and provide a sense of connection and commonality in a world of anguish and uncertainty. Music can and will contribute to our efforts to find common ground and, ultimately, peace.

Finally, while we all have a responsibility to *bear witness* to the events of the world around us, for musicians and artists, that responsibility is far more fundamental. It is the essence of what they do. Legendary musician and activist Nina Simone articulated this well. "You can't help it. An artist's duty is to reflect the times."

To that end, we pledge to encourage and provide a platform, through our events and programs, for musicians and artists to continue to bear witness to racism, injustice and inequality.

There is no better song to sharpen that point than, "Strange Fruit." Written as a protest to the inhumanity of racism, it was penned and arranged by Abel Meeropol, a white Jewish man from the Bronx after seeing a picture of a lynching. Billie Holiday recorded the song in 1939.

*Southern trees bear a strange fruit.*
*Blood on the leaves and blood on the root.*
*Black body swinging in the Southern breeze.*
*Strange fruit hanging from the poplar trees.*
*Pastoral scene of the gallant South.*
*The bulging eyes and the twisted mouth.*
*Scent of magnolia sweet and fresh.*
*And the sudden smell of burning flesh.*
*Here is a fruit for the crows to pluck.*
*For the rain to gather, for the wind to suck.*
*For the sun to rot, for a tree to drop.*
*Here is a strange and bitter crop*

The power and truth of that song still applies today. And it is the reason why we need artists and musicians to continue to reflect the times. To learn more about the history of this song, visit: https://www. youtube.com/watch?v=EZUoYgPe1Y4

MFE has been consistently working to cultivate the power of music as an educational, community building and public health tool for fifteen years. But we must do more. And we will. In times like these cultivating music's power as a tool to educate, build community, heal and yes, to bear witness to racism, injustice and inequality is more important than ever.

Please join us as we all must do more. The future of our community depends upon it.

Let's keep singing . . . in harmony . . . together.

# ACKNOWLEDGMENTS

There have been so many people, family, old friends and some new friends who have contributed to this project. There are simply too many to list them all.

That said, there are a few who bear special mention. Thank you, Michael Coffino for your sharp editorial eye, particularly as it related to the general organization of the content. I have also greatly appreciated your helpful advice on how to navigate the often crazy and rapidly changing publishing process and industry. Your consistent encouragement was also greatly appreciated.

A big thank you to Shasta Clinch for her very helpful and informative DEI/Sensitivity read.

I am also profoundly grateful for the time, effort, and emotion that each of the nine essayists (Le Hinton, Amy Banks, Terian Mack, Madison DeWispelaere, Tony Collins, Kevin Ressler, Dr. Leroy Hopkins, Fran Rodriguez, and Dom Jordan) poured into their contributions that appeared in the "Voices to be Heard" chapter. You all have made this book infinitely more powerful.

To Rich Perkey, friend, former teammate, and fellow writer for our many discussions, not only about the content contained within, but also about the writing process itself. My brothers Greg and Tom and sister Jeannie should be mentioned as they have helped shape my perspective around these issues for a lifetime. I've cherished their support, encouragement, and love.

There are several others who deserve special mention as they have all influenced my thinking and perspective on these issues and this project. Again, there are too many to mention, but in particular, I am grateful to Deb Rohrer, Tony Collins, Kevin Ressler, Steve Chambers,

Joey McMonagle, Michael Jamanis, Amanda Kemp, and Jim Morrissey.

To John Koehler for believing in this project and for his encouragement and guidance. To Joe Coccaro for his editorial eye, and Lauren Sheldon for her work on conceptualizing and organizing the book cover design and selection process.

Finally, to my parents, Polly and Steve Gerdy, who were very clear from the start that everyone, regardless of color or standing in life, deserves respect and that intolerance would simply not be tolerated in our household.

# BIBLIOGRAPHY AND REFERENCES

Alexander, Michelle. *The New Jim Crow: Mass Incarceration in the Age of Colorblindness.* (New York, London: The New Press, 2020).

Baldwin, James. *The Fire Next Time* (New York: Vintage International, 1993. Copyright 1962 by James Baldwin).

Benedict, Marie and Murray, Victoria Christopher. *The Personal Librarian* (New York: Berkley, 2021)

Berry, Wendall. *The Hidden Wound.* (Berkeley: Counterpoint, 1989, 2010)

Blight, David W. *Frederick Douglass: Prophet of Freedom* (New York: Simon and Schuster Paperbacks, 2018)

Butler, Anthea. White *Evangelical Racism: The Politics of Morality in America* (Chapel Hill, NC: The University of North Carolina Press, 2021)

*Caste: A Brief History* (University Press, 2020).

Coates, Ta-Nehisi. *Between the World and Me* (New York: Spiegel and Grau, 2015).

Dennis, David, Jr. in collaboration with David Dennis, Sr. *The Movement Made Us: A Father, A Son, and the Legacy of a Freedom Ride.* (New York: HarperCollins Publishers, 2022)

DiAngelo, Robin. *Nice Racism: How Progressive White People Perpetuate Racial Harm* (Boston, MA: Beacon Press, 2021).

DiAngelo, Robin. *White Fragility: Why It's So Hard for White People to Talk About Racism* (Boston, MA: Beacon Press, 2018).

DuBois, W.E.B. *The Soul of Black Folk* (Mineola, NY: Dover Publications, Inc., 1994).

Dyson, Michael Eric. *Tears We Cannot Stop: A Sermon to White America* (New York: St. Martin's Press, 2017, 2021).

Feinstein, John. *Raise a Fist, Take a Knee: Race and the Illusion of Progress in Modern Sports.* (New York: Little, Brown and Company, 2021) .

Glaude, Eddie S. Jr. *Begin Again: James Baldwin's America and Its Urgent Lessons for Our Own* (New York: Crown, 2020).

Gonzalez, Juan. *Harvest of Empire: A History of Latinos in America* (New York: Penguin Books, 2001, 2011).

Hannah-Jones, Nikole. *The 1619 Project: A New Origin Story.* (New York: One World, 2021).

Hurston, Zora Neale. *Barracoon: The Story of the Last "Black Cargo"* (New York: Amistad, 2018).

Kendi, Ibrahm X. *How to be an Anti-Racist* (New York: One World, 2019).

Kendi, Ibrahm X., and Blain, Keisha N. *Four Hundred Souls: A Community History of African America, 1619 – 2019* (New York: One World, 2021).

Kendi, Ibrahm X. *Stamped From the Beginning: The Definitive History of Racist Ideas in America* (New York: Bold Type Books, 2016).

King, Jr., Martin Luther. *Where Do We Go from Here: Chaos or Community?* (Boston, MA: Beacon Press, 1968).

Loewen, James W. *Lies My Teacher Told Me: Everything Your American History Textbook Got Wrong* (New York, London: The New Press, 1995, 2007, 2018).

Magness, Phillip W. *The 1619 Project: A Critique*. (American Institute for Economic Research, 2020).

McGhee, Heather. *The Sum of Us: What Racism Costs Everyone and How We Can Prosper Together* (New York: One World, 2021).

Meacham, Jon. *His Truth is Marching on: John Lewis and the Power of Hope* (New York: Random House, 2020).

*New York Times Magazine*. Homans, Charles, "Made in America: How a new era of political violence arrived on the streets of Kenosha, Wisconsin": (Sunday, October 31, 2021).

Picoult, Jodi. *Small Great Things* (New York: Ballantine Press, 2016).

Ross, Dax-Devlon. *Letters to My White Male Friends* (New York: St. Martin's Press, 2021).

Rothstein, Richard. *The Color of Law: A Forgotten History of How Our Government Segregated America* (New York, London: Liveright Publishing Corporation, 2017).

Saad, Layla F. *Me and White Supremacy: Combat Racism, Change the World, and Become a Good Ancestor* (Naperville, IL.: Sourcebooks, 2020).

Smith, Clint. *How the Word is Passed: A Reckoning with the History of Slavery Across America* (New York, Boston, London: Little, Brown and Company, 2021)

Smith, Lillian. *Killers of the Dream* (New York, London: W. W. Norton & Company, 1949, 1961).

Wells, Ida B. *Crusade for Justice: The Autobiography of Ida B. Wells* (Chicago, Illinois: University of Chicago Press, 1970, 2020)

West, Cornel. *Race Matters; 25th Anniversary* (Boston: Beacon Press, 2017).

West, Cornel. *Democracy Matters: Winning the Fight Against Imperialism* (New York: Penguin Books, 2005).

Wilkerson, Isabel. *The Warmth of Other Suns: The Epic Story of America's Great Migration* (New York: Vintage Books, 2010).

Wise, Tim. *Reflections on Race From a Privileged Son* (Berkeley, CA: Soft Skull Press, 2008, 2011)

Woodward, C. Vann. *The Strange Career of Jim Crow* (New York: Oxford University Press, 2002).

Young, Kevin, Editor. *African American Poetry: 250 Years of Struggle and Song* (New York: Literary Classics of the United States, Inc., 2020).

# A NOTE ON QUOTES TO OPEN CHAPTERS

**M**y process for identifying the quotes used at the beginning of each chapter was to Google search for websites that list various quotes related to particular ideas or themes. In this case, relating to the various themes explored in each chapter. I used websites such as BrainyQuotes.com, HeartstoMind.org, Kidadl.com, InspiringQuotes. us, Quotemaster.org, GoodReads.com, and AZQuotes.com.